The Cabala

The Cabala

Its Influence on
Judaism and Christianity

Bernhard Pick

Open Court
La Salle, Illinois

Publisher's Note

This 1974 Open Court Paperback edition is an un-
abridged reproduction of the 1913 Open Court
clothbound edition.

ISBN: 0-87548-199-X
LCCN: 13-26188

CONTENTS

The Cabala

THE CABALA.

Foreword.—Although the Cabala belongs to the past, it nevertheless demands our attention on account of the interest taken in it by men like Raymond Lully, the "Doctor Illuminatus" as he was styled (died 1315): John Picus di Mirandola (1463-1494); John Reuchlin (1455-1522); Cornelius Henry Agrippa von Nettesheim (1486-1535); John Baptist von Helmont (1577-1644); the English scholars Robert Fludd (1574-1637) and Henry More (1614-1687). How much Theophrastus Paracelsus (1493-1541) and Jacob Boehme (1575-1624), called "Philosophus Teutonicus," were influenced by cabalistic doctrines, is difficult to state. At any rate the names mentioned before are sufficient to call attention to a theosophical system which has engaged the minds of Jewish and Christian scholars.

It is surprising how scanty the English literature is on the Cabala. True that in the *History of the Jews* by Basnage, London, 1708, we have a lengthy account of this theosophy (pp. 184-256); but this account is originally given in the French work *Histoire des Juifs,* by the same author. John Gill (died 1771) in his *"Dissertatio de genuina Punctorum Vocalium Hebraicorum Antiquitate, contra Cappellum, Waltonum,"* etc., prefixed to his *Clavis Pentateuchi,* Edinburgh, 1770, refers to the Zohar to prove the antiquity of the Hebrew vowel-points, because it states that "the vowel-points proceeded from the Holy Spirit who indited the Sacred Scriptures," etc. (on Song of Songs 57*b;* ed. Amsterdam, 1701). Of course so long as the Cabala was believed to be a genuine revelation from God, and Simon ben Jochai (of the second century)' was believed to be the author of the Zohar, to whom God communicated all the mysteries, it was but a matter of course to believe in the antiquity and divinity of the vowel-points.

John Allen (died 1839) in his *Modern Judaism,* London, 1816, (2d. ed. 1830) also gives an account of the Cabala, in which he premises the antiquity of the Zohar, which he makes the primary source of the primitve Cabala. Passing over Dean Milman's (died 1868) *History of the Jews,* London, 1829, (often reprinted), in which we naturally also find references to the Cabala, we mention J. W. Etheridge (died 1866), author of *Jerusalem and Tiberias; Sora and Cordova, a*

Survey of the Religious and Scholastic Learning of the Jews, Designed as an Introduction to Hebrew Literature, London, 1856. This author seems to have been acquainted with the researches of the Jewish scholars in Germany, but he nevertheless stoutly adheres to the traditional view. Thus he remarks on page 314:

"To the authenticity of the Zohar, as a work of the early Kabalistic school, objections have indeed been made, but they are not of sufficient gravity to merit an extended investigation. The opinion that ascribes it as a pseudo-fabrication to Moses de Leon in the thirteenth century, has, I imagine, but few believers among the learned in this subject in our own day. The references to Shemun ben Yochaï and the Kabala in the Talmud, and abundant internal evidence found in the book itself, exhibit the strongest probability, not that Shemun himself was the author of it, but that it is the fruit and result of his personal instructions, and of the studies of his immediate disciples."

We may say that Etheridge's view is *mutatis mutandis* also that of Ad. Franck, author of *Système de la Kabbale ou la philosophie religieuse des Hebreux,* Paris, 1843 (2d. ed. 1892); translated into German by A. Gelinek (Jellinek), *Die Kabbala oder die Religionsphilosophie der Hebräer,* Leipsig, 1844, with which must be com-

5

pared D. H. Joel, *Die Religionsphilosophie des Sohar, ibid.*, 1840, which is an exceedingly good supplement to Franck's work. But an examination of the works published by Zunz, *Die gottesdienstlichen Vorträge der Juden*, Berlin, 1831, p. 405; Geiger, *Melo Chofnayim, ibid.*, 1840, introduction, p. xvii; Sachs, *Die religiöse Poesie der Juden in Spanien, ibid.*, 1845, p. 327, Jellinek, *Moses Ben Schem Tob de Leon*, Leipsig, 1851, could have convinced Etheridge that the Zohar, the text-book of the Cabala, is the "pseudo-fabrication" of Moses de Leon in the thirteenth century. That Landauer (died 1841) in his essays on the Cabala published in the *Litteraturblatt des Orients*, 1845, p. 178 et seq., 1846, p. 12 et seq., ascribes the authorship of the Zohar to Abraham ben Samuel Abulafia towards the end of the second half of the thirteenth century, is the more weighty and instructive because he originally started with opinions of an exactly opposite character (Steinschneider, *Jewish Literature*, p. 299). Nevertheless Etheridge's book was a good work; it was the praiseworthy attempt of an English Christian to acquaint the English-speaking people with the post-Biblical literature of the Jews.

Four years after the publication of the above work, Canon Westcott (died 1901) published his *Introduction to the Study of the Gospels*, London, 1860, in which he incidentally refers to the Cabala, without adopting Etheridge's view as to the authorship of the Zohar; on the contrary he says (p. 159, Boston, 1867): "The Sepher ha-Zohar, or Book of Splendor, owes its existence to R. Moses of Leon in the thirteenth century," and this, he says in a note, "has been satisfactorily established by Jellinek in his tract, *Moses ben Schemtob de Leon und sein Verhältniss zum Sohar,* Leipsig, 1851. The warm approval of Jost is sufficient to remove any lingering doubt as to the correctness of Jellinek's conclusion: *A Jellinek und die Kabala,* Leipsic, 1852."

The publication of Jellinek's *Beiträge zur Geschichte der Kabbala,* 2 parts, Leipsic, 1852; and his *Auswahl kabbalistischer Mystik,* part I, *ibid.,* 1853; Stern's "Versuch einer umständlichen Analyse des Sohar" (in *Ben Chananja, Monatsschrift für jüdische Theologie,* Vols. I-IV, Szegedin, 1858-1861); Jost's *Geschichte des Judenthums und seiner Sekten,* Vol. III, pp. 66-81, Leipsic, 1859; more especially of Graetz's *Geschichte der Juden,*[1] Vol. VII, pp. 73-87, 442-459; 487-507, Leipsic, 1863, paved the way for Christian D. Ginsburg's (now very scarce) essay

---

[1] The English translation of this work, published by the Jewish Publication Society of America, is of no service to the student, because the scholarly notes, which are the best part of the original, are entirely omitted.

The Kabbalah, London, 1865. As a matter of course he adopts the results of modern scholarship and rejects the authorship of Simon ben Jochaî.

As far as we are aware, nothing has been published in English since 1865. *The Kabbalah Unveiled* by S. L. M. Mathers, London, 1887, gives only a translation of some parts of the Zohar, which Knorr von Rosenroth had rendered into Latin. Nevertheless this work is interesting, because an English reader—provided he has enough patience—can get a taste of the Zoharic wisdom and unwisdom.

CHAPTER I.

NAME AND ORIGIN OF THE CABALA.

The Cabala.—By Cabala we understand that system of religious philosophy, or more properly, of Jewish theosophy, which played so important a part in the theological and exegetical literature of both Jews and Christians ever since the Middle Ages.

The Hebrew word Cabala (from Kibbel) properly denotes "reception," then "a doctrine received by oral tradition." The term is thus in itself nearly equivalent to "transmission," like the Latin *traditio,* in Hebrew *masorah,* for which last, indeed, the Talmud makes it interchangeable in the statement given in Pirke Abot I, 1: "Moses received (*kibbel*) the Law on Mount Sinai, and transmitted (*umsarah*) it to Joshua." The difference, however, between the word "Cabala" and the cognate term *masorah* is that the former expressed "the act of receiving," while the latter denotes "the act of giving over, surrendering, transmitting." The name, therefore,

9

tells us no more than that this theosophy has
been received traditionally. In the oldest Jewish
literature (Mishna, Midrash, Talmud), the Cabala denotes the whole body of Jewish tradition.
The name is even applied to the prophetic writings of the Old Testament, and the Hagiographa,
in contradistinction to the Pentateuch. As a
scientific system the Cabala is also called *chokmat
ha-cabalah,* i. e., science of tradition, or *chokmah
nistarah* (abbreviated *ch'n,* i. e., *chen,* חן), i. e.,
secret science or wisdom, and its representatives
and adherents delighted in calling themselves
maskilim, i. e., "intelligent," or with a play of
words *yodé ch'n,* i. e., "connoisseurs of secret
wisdom."

Having defined the term Cabala, which was
still commonly used for "oral tradition" in the
13th and 14th centuries even after the technical
sense of the word was established, we must be
careful to distinguish between cabala and mysticism. Like other Eastern nations, the Jews
were naturally inclined to theosophical specula-
tion and though this tendency may have been re-
pressed by the definite teaching of revelation as
long as they were confined within the sacred
boundaries of Palestine, it found a freer scope
after the Exile.

There were two subjects about which the
Jewish imagination especially busied itself,—the

history of the Creation, and the *Merkabah,* or the Divine apparition to Ezekiel. Both touch the question of God's original connection with His creatures, and that of His continued intercourse with them. They treat of the mystery of nature and of Providence, especially of Revelation; and an attempt is made to answer the question, how the Infinite God can have any connection or intercourse with finite creatures.

It is difficult to say how far it is possible to trace with certainty Jewish mysticism. Even in the book of Sirach (Ecclus, xlix. 8) it is the special praise of Ezekiel that he saw the chariot of the Cherubim. When we come to the period of the Mishna, we find the existence of a body of esoteric doctrine already presupposed. It is laid down that "no one ought to discourse the history of Creation (Gen. i) with two, or the Chariot (Ezek. i) with one, unless he be a scholar, who has knowledge of his own" (Chagiga II, 1).

Further allusions to these mysterious doctrines occur in the Talmud, but any rash investigation of them was discouraged, as is shown by the story of the four sages in "the enclosed garden," i. e., who were engaged in theosophical studies. One of them, it was said, had looked around and died; another had looked around and lost his reason; a third eventually tried to destroy the garden;[1] while the fourth alone had entered and returned in safety (Chagiga, fol. 14, col. 2).

Little by little mysticism made its way from Palestine into Babylonia and found many followers. Its adepts called themselves "Men of Faith." They boasted of possessing the means of obtaining a view of the divine household. By virtue of certain incantations, invocations of the names of God and the angels, and the recitation of certain prayer-like chants, combined with fasting and an ascetic mode of living, they pretended to be able to perform supernatural deeds. For this purpose they made use of amulets and cameos (*Kameoth*), and wrote upon them the names of God and the angels with certain signs. Miracle-working was a trifle to these mystics. The books which they wrote only gave hints, and only those were initiated into the mystic secrets, in whose hand and forehead the adepts pretended to discover lines that proved them to be worthy of being initiated.

Origin of the Cabala.—Deferring until later

[1] In the Talmud he is called Elisha ben-Abuja, surnamed Acher, i. e., "the other one," after his apostasy from Judaism. It is related of him that while attending the Jewish college he had often been noticed to carry with him writings of the "Minim" (probably of Gnostics), and that he had even been in the habit of quoting Greek poetry. Elisha was a pupil of the famous rabbi Akiba; comp. Jellinek, *Elisha ben-Abujja, genannt Acher,* Leipsic, 1847.

the works belonging to this period, we will now speak of the origin of the Cabala. Although the name "Cabala" in its pregnant meaning is first used in the 13th century, yet Jewish tradition claims a high antiquity for the Cabala and traces it back, among others, to three famous Talmudists, as the proper founders of the Cabala, viz., Rabbi Ismaël ben Elisa (about 121 A. D.) ; Nechunjah Ben-Ha-Kanah (about 70 A. D.), and especially Simon ben Jochaï (about 150 A. D.),[2] the reputed author of the Zohar.

Whatever may be the claims of these traditions they must be rejected. The mystical speculations of the Cabala are entirely foreign to older Judaism, especially original Mosaism. It is true that the Talmud contains many things concerning God, heaven, hell, world, magic, etc.,[3] but these things were generally assigned to some individuals, and are elements derived from Parsism and neo-Platonism; and much as the Talmud and Midrash may otherwise speak of the three teachers mentioned before, such things are not recorded of them. The Cabala as a mystical system and its development as such undoubtedly belongs to the Middle Ages, beginning probably with the seventh century of our era, and culmin-

[2] See my article *s. v.* in McClintock and Strong's *Cyclop.*, Vol. IX, p. 757.

[3] The reader is referred for such things to my article "Talmud," *loc. cit.*, Vol. X, pp. 170, 171.

ating in the Book Zohar. A fuller and more mature development of the Cabala is due to the speculations of later masters.

The origin of the Cabala belongs to that period in which Judaism on the one hand was permeated by a crude anthropomorphic notion of the Deity, whereas on the other hand Platonism and Aristotelianism strove for the ascendency in formulating the fundamental doctrines of Jewish belief. With Moses Maimonides (1135-1204) rationalism had reached its climax. The injunctions of the Bible were only to be explained by the light of reason. Only the simple, primary or literary sense (*peshat*) of the Scripture was recognized, the existing allegorical interpretation (*derúsh*) was considered either as rabbinical fancy, or one saw in it only a poetical form. Even the Talmud had been systematized and codified. Religion had become a more or less meaningless *opus operatum*. Philosophy had always been treated as something secondary, which had nothing to do with practical Judaism, as it is daily and hourly practiced. Maimonides, on the other hand, had introduced it into the holiest place in Judaism, and, as it were, gave Aristotle a place next to the doctors of the Law. Instead of unifying Judaism, Maimonides caused a division, and the Maimunists and Anti-Maimunists opposed each other. A reaction came and the

Cabala stepped in as a counterpoise to the growing shallowness of the Maimunists' philosophy. The storm against his system broke out in Provence and spread over Spain. The latter country may be considered as the real home of the Cabala. When the Jews were driven from that country, the Cabala took root in Palestine and thence it was carried back into the different countries of Europe.

The fundamental ideas of the Cabala are unJewish, derived from Philo, the neo-Platonists and the neo-Pythagoreans; we sometimes even notice Gnostic influences. But the close amalgamation of these different elements with Biblical and Midrashic ideas has given to these foreign parts such a Jewish coloring, that at the first glance they appear as an emanation of the Jewish mental life.

CHAPTER II.

THE DEVELOPMENT OF THE CABALA IN THE PRE-ZOHAR PERIOD.

Pre-Zohar Period.—The history of the Cabala comprises a period of nearly a thousand years. Its beginning may be traced back to the seventh century, whereas its last shoots belong to the eighteenth century. For convenience' sake we can distinguish two periods, the one reaching from the seventh to the thirteenth century, the other from the fourteenth to the eighteenth century. The former is the time of gradual growth, development and progress, the other that of decline and decay. The origin of the Zohar in the thirteenth century forms the climax in the history of the Cabala. It became the treasury to the followers of this theosophy, a text-book for the students of the Cabala, the standard and code of the cabalistic system, the Bible of the Cabalists.

From the seventh to the ninth century we meet with the representatives of the mysteries of the *merkaba*,[1] which is expounded in the so-called *Hekaloth*, i. e., "Palaces." This work, which is ascribed to Ismaël ben-Elisa, opens with a description of God's throne and his household consisting of angelic hosts. In this mystical production, which has been reprinted by Jellinek in *Bet ha-Midrash*, Vol. III, pp. 83-108, the praises of the Almighty God and his chariot throne are celebrated. We are told that each of the seven heavenly palaces is guarded by eight angels; a description of the formula is given by virtue of which these angelic guards are obliged to grant admission into the celestial palaces; also a description of the peculiar qualifications necessary for those who desire to enter into these palaces. Some hymns of praise and a conversation with God, Israel and the angels conclude this treatise, which like the *Shiur Koma* or the treatise on "the Dimensions of the Deity," also ascribed to Rabbi Ismaël, knows nothing of the speculations of the En Soph, the ten Sephiroth and the doctrine of the Transmigration of Souls.

Another work belonging to this period is the

[1]*Merkaba*, i. e., "Chariot," mentioned in Ezek. i and x, which treat of the Divine Throne, resting on wheels, and carried by sacred animals. Great mysteries are attached by the ancient Jews to all details of this description of the Deity and his surroundings, which in imitation of *Maasey Bereshit*, i. e., "the work of the hexahemeron" or "cosmogony," is also called *Maasey Merkaba*, "the Work of the Chariot," a kind of "theosophy."

Othijoth de Rabbi Akiba, i. e., "the Alphabet of
Rabbi Akiba," which alternately treats each letter of the Hebrew alphabet "as representing an
idea as an abbreviation for a word, and as the
symbol of some sentiment, according to its peculiar form, in order to attach to those letters
moral, theoanthropic, angelological and mystical
notions." This treatise is also given in Jellinek's
work, cited above, Vol. III, pp. 12-49, Leipsic,
1855. A Latin translation of Akiba's Alphabet
is given by Kircher, in his *Œdipus Ægyptiacus,*[2]
and in Bartolocci's *Bibliotheca Rabbinica.*[3]

Bodenschatz in his *Kirchliche Verfassung der
heutigen Juden,* (Erlangen, 1748) gives in Part
III, p. 15, the following specimen: "On the
words: 'The Lord is nigh unto them that are
of a broken heart' (Ps. xxxiv, 18) we read: 'All
who are of a broken heart are more agreeable before God than the ministering angels, because the
ministering angels are remote from the divine
Majesty 360,000,000 miles, as it is said in Is. vi.
2: "Above it stood the Seraphim" (*mimaal lo*),
where the word *lo* by way of gematria means
36,000. This teaches us that the body of the
divine Majesty is 2,000,000,336,000 miles long.
From his loins upward are 1,000,000,180,000
miles, and from his loins downward 118 times
10,000 miles. But these miles are not like ours,

[2] Rome, 1652, Vol. II, p. 225 f.
[3] Vol. IV, pp. 27 f.

but like his (God's) miles. For his mile is 1,000,000 ells long, and his ell contains four spans and a hand's breadth, and his span goes from one end of the world to the other, as is said Is. x. 12: "Who has measured the waters in the hollow of his hand, and meted out heaven with the span?" Another explanation is that the words "and meted out heaven with the span" denote that the heaven and the heaven of all heavens is only one span long, wide and high, and that the earth with all the abysses is as long as the sole of the foot, and wide as the sole of the foot, etc., etc.' "

Another part of Akiba's Alphabet is the so-called "Book of Enoch,"[4] which describes the glorification of Enoch and his transformation into the angel Metatron, regarding him as "the little God" in contradistinction to "the Great God."

These mystical treatises came into existence in the course of time, and their teachings rapidly spread. So numerous became the disciples of mysticism in the twelfth century that Maimonides found it necessary to denounce the system. "Give no credence to the nonsense of the writers of charms and amulets, to what they tell you or to what you find in their foolish writings about the divine names; which they invent without any

[4] Also reprinted in Jellinek's *Bet Ha-Midrash,* Vol. II, pp. 114-117.

sense, calling them appellations of the Deity, and affirming that they require holiness and purity and perform miracles. All these things are fables; a sensible man will not listen to them, much less believe in them."[5]

A new stage in the development of the Cabala commences with the publication of *The Book of Creation or Jezirah,* which is the first work that comprises the philosophical speculations of the age in one systematic whole. Scholars are now agreed that the Book of Jezirah belongs to the eighth or ninth centuries, and that it has nothing to do with the Jezirah-Book mentioned in the Talmud, where we are told that "Rabbis Hanina and Oshaya studied it every Friday, whereby they produced a calf three years old and ate it" (*Sanhedrin,* fol. 65, col. 2), and whereby Rabbi Joshua ben Hananya declared he could take fruit and instantly produce the trees which belong to them (*Jerusalem Sanhedrin,* chapt. VII towards the end).[6]

[5] More, *Nebuchim* I, 61. Wünsche thinks that the treatise *De Judaicis süperstitionibus* by Agobard, bishop of Lyons (died 840), was directed against this mystic tendency.

[6] L. Goldschmidt, *Das Buch der Schöpfung,* Frankfurt a. M., 1894, p. 10, remarks: "I am inclined to put the time of the composition of the Book Jezirah into the second century B. C., and assert that it is the same book of the Creation which is mentioned in the Talmud." He is also inclined to make Palestine the place of its composition.

The Sepher Jezirah as we now have it, is properly a monologue on the part of Abraham, in which, by the contemplation of all that is around him, he ultimately arrived at the conviction of the Unity of God. Hence the remark of the philosopher Jehudah Halevi (born about 1086)—"the Book of the Creation, which belongs to our father Abraham . . . . . . demonstrates the existence of the Deity and the Divine Unity, by things which are on the one hand manifold and multifarious, whilst on the other hand they converge and harmonize; and this harmony can only proceed from One who originated it" (*Khozari*, IV, 25).

Referring the reader to the literature on the Sepher Jezirah to Goldschmidt's book, pp. 35-46,[7] we will state that the Book of Creation consists of six *Perakim* or chapters, subdivided into thirty-three very brief *Mishnahs* or sections, as follows: the first chapter has twelve sections, the second has five, the third five, the fourth four, the fifth three, and the sixth four sections. The doctrines which the book propounds are delivered in the style of aphorisms or theorems, and, pretending to be the dicta of Abraham, are laid down very dogmatically, in a manner becoming the authority of this patriarch, who, ac-

[7] We may add the English translation of the book by Edersheim, *The Life and Times of Jesus the Messiah*, Vol. II (1883), pp. 690-695.

21

cording to Artapanus instructed King Phare-
thothes of Egypt in astrology (Eusebius, *Praep.
evang.*, IX, 18); fulfilled the whole law, before
it was given (*Apoc. Baruch,* chap. 57; *Kiddu-
shin,* IV, 14 fin.), and victoriously overcame ten
temptations[8] (*Pirke Aboth,* V, 3).

Theosophical Arithmetic.—The book opens
with the statement that "by thirty-two paths of
secret wisdom, the Eternal, the Lord of Hosts, the
God of Israel the living God, the King of the Universe, the Merciful and Gracious, the High and
Exalted God, He who inhabits eternity, Glorious
and Holy is His name, hath created the world by
means of number, word and writing (or number,
numberer, numbered)" I. 1.—The book shows
why there are just thirty-two of these. By an
analysis of this number it seeks to exhibit, in a
peculiar method of theosophical arithmetic, on
the assumption that they are the signs of existence and thought, the doctrine that God produced
all, and is over all, the universe being a development of original entity, and existence being but
thought become concrete; "in short, that instead
of the heathenish or popular Jewish conception
of the world as outward, or co-existent with De-

[8] Comp. in general Beer, *Leben Abraham's nach
Auffassung der jüdischen Sage,* Leipsic, 1859; Grünbaum, *Neue Beiträge zur semitischen Sagenkunde;*
1893, pp. 89-132; Bonwetsch, *Die Apokalypse Abrahams,*
1897, pp. 41-55.

ity, it is co-equal in birth, having been brought out of nothing by God, thus establishing a Pantheistic system of emanation, of which, principally because it is not anywhere designated by name, one would think the writer was not himself quite conscious."

The following will illustrate the curious proof of this argumentation: the number 32 is the sum of 10, the number of the ten fingers (I, 3), and 22, the number of the Hebrew alphabet, this latter being afterwards further resolved into 3+7+12 (I, 2). The first chapter (I, 2-8 treats of the decade and its elements, which are called figures in contradistinction from the 22 letters. This decade is the sign-manual of the universe. In the details of this hypothesis the existence of divinity in the abstract is really ignored, though not formally denied. Thus the number *one* is its spirit as an active principle, in which all worlds and beings are yet enclosed. "One is the spirit of the living God, blessed and again blessed be the Name of Him, Who liveth for ever— Voice and Spirit and Word, and this is the Holy Ghost" (I, 9).

Two is the spirit from this spirit, i. e., the active principle in so far as it has beforehand decided on creating; "in it He engraved the twenty-two letters" (I, 10).

Three is water; *four* is fire; "in it He hewed

the throne of glory, the Ophanim[9] and Seraphim, the sacred living creatures, and the angels of service, and of these three He founded His dwelling place, as it is said, He maketh His angels breaths, and His ministers a flaming fire (I, 11, 12). The six remaining figures, 5-10, are regarded severally as the sign-manual of height, depth, east, west, north and south, forming the six sides of a cube, and representing the idea of form in its geometrical perfection (I, 13).

In the words of the Book of Creation the hexade is thus described: *"Five*: Three letters from out the simple ones; He sealed spirit on the three, and fastened them in His great Name J H V.[10] And He sealed with them six outgoings (ends, terminations); He turned upwards, and He sealed it with J H V. *Six*: He sealed below, turned downwards, and sealed it with J V H. *Seven*: He sealed eastward, He turned in front of Him, and sealed it with H J V. *Eight*: He sealed westward and turned behind, and sealed it with H V J. *Nine*: He sealed southward, and turned to His right, and sealed it with V J H. *Ten*: He sealed northward, and turned to His left, and sealed it with V H J. These are the Sephiroth: (1) Spirit of the living God, and (2)

---

[9] Ophanim (אופנים, plural of אופן), translated "wheels" in the English version (Ezek. i. 20), is taken by the Jewish Rabbis to denote "a distinct order of angels," just as Cherubim and Seraphim. Hence the

wind [air or spirit?][11] (3) water, and (4) fire; and (5) height above and (6) below, (7) east and (8) west, (9) north and (10) south."

[*Sephiroth* is the plural of the word *Sephirah*. Azariel derives the word from *saphar*, "to number"; later Cabalists derive it either from *saphir*, "Saphir," or from the Greek "spheres,"[12] and are not at all certain whether to regard the Sephiroth as "principles,"[13] or as "substances,"[14] or as "potencies, powers,"[15] or as "intelligent worlds,"[16] or as "attributes," or as "entities,"[17] or as "organs of the Deity" (*Kelim*). We might fairly well translate the word *Sephiroth* by "emanations."]

We see, however, that this alone establishes

Talmudic explanation of Exod. xx, 20, by "Thou shalt not make the likeness of those ministering servants who serve before me in heaven, viz., Ophanim, Seraphim, sacred Chajoth and missive angels," (*Rosh ha-Shana*, fol. 24, clo. 2). *Ophan*, the prince of this order, is regarded by the ancient sages as identical with the angel *Sandalphon*, סנדלפון = συνάδελφος, co-brother or fellow-companion of the angel Metabron.

[10] These three letters mean Jahu, or Yahveh, now pronounced Jehovah, of which they are the abbreviation; what follows shows how the permutation of these three letters marks the varied relationship of God to creation in time and space, and at the same time, so to speak, the immanence of His manifestation in it.

[11] The word *ruach* means all these.

[12] σφαῖραι.

[13] ἀρχαί.

[14] ὑποστάσεις.

[15] δυνάμεις.

[16] κόσμοι νοητικοί.

[17] *Azamoth*.

nothing real, but merely expounds the idea of possibility or actuality, at the same time establishing that which is *virtualiter* as really existing in God, the foundation of all things, from which the whole universe proceeded. The actual entities are therefore introduced in the subsequent chapters under the twenty-two letters. The connection between the two series is evidently the Word, which in the first Sephira (number) is yet identical in voice and action with the spirit (I, 9); but afterwards these elements, separating as creator and substance, together produce the world, the materials of which are represented by the letters, severally divided into gutturals, labials, palatals, linguals and dentals (II, 3), since these by their manifold manifestations, name and describe all that exists.

These twenty-two letters of the alphabet are then divided into three groups, consisting respectively of:

1. The three mothers or fundamental letters (ch. III);

2. Seven double (ch. IV), and

3. Twelve simple consonants (ch. V).

First are subtracted from the twenty-two letters the three mothers (Aleph, Mem, Shin), i. e., the universal relations of (1) principle, (2) contrary principle, and (3) balance (i. e., the intermediate)..

In the world. we have air, water, fire. This

	means, the heavens are from fire, the earth from water, and the air indicates the intermediate between the fire and the water.
In the year..	there is fire, and water, and wind. The heat comes from fire, cold from water, and moderation from wind (air) that is intermediate between them.
In man.....	there is fire, water and wind. The head is from fire, the belly from water, and the body from wind that is intermediate between them.

The three mothers or fundamental letters are followed by the seven duplicate letters—Beth, Gimel, Daleth, Caph, Pe, Resh, Tau[18]—duplicate, because they are opposite as life and death; peace and evil; wisdom and folly; riches and poverty; grace and ugliness; fertility and desolation; rule and servitude (IV, 1): These seven duplicate letters correspond to the seven outgoings: above and below, east and west, north and south, and the holy Temple in the middle, and it upbears the whole (IV, 2). From them God created:

[18] These letters of the Hebrew Alphabet are called double because they have a double pronunciation, being sometimes aspirated and sometimes not, according to their being with or without the *dagesh* (i. e., a point in the middle).

27

In the world. Saturn, Jupiter, Mars, Sun, Venus, Mercury, Moon.

In man...... Wisdom, Riches, Dominion, Life, Favor, Progeny, Peace.

In the year.. Sabbath, Thursday, Tuesday, Sunday, Friday, Wednesday, Monday.

With these seven letters God also formed the seven heavens, the seven earths or countries, and the seven weeks from the feast of Passover to Pentecost (IV, 3, 4). These letters also represent the seven gates of issue in the soul; two eyes, two ears, and a mouth, and the two nostrils.

Turning finally to the twelve single letters (ch. V), they show the relations of things so far as they can be apprehended in a universal category. By means of these twelve letters God created the twelve signs of the zodiac, viz.:

In the world. Aries, Taurus, Gemini, Cancer, Leo, Virgo, Libra, Scorpio, Sagittarius, Capricornus, Aquarius, Pisces.

In the year.. the twelve months, viz.: Nisan, Ijar, Sivan, Tamus, Ab, Elul, Tishri, Cheshvan or Marcheshvan, Kislev, Tebet, Shebat, Adar.

In man ..... the organs of sight, hearing, smelling, talking, taste, copulating, dealing, walking, thinking, anger, laughter, sleeping (ch. V, 1).

They are so organized by God as to form at once a province, and yet be ready for battle, i. e., they are as well fitted for harmonious as for dissentious action. "God has placed in all things one to oppose the other; good to oppose evil, good to proceed from good, and evil from evil; good to purify evil, and evil to purify good; the good is in store for the good, and the evil is reserved for the evil" (VI, 2). "The twelve are arranged against each other in battle array; three serve love, three hatred; three engender life, and three death. The three loving ones are the heart, the ears and the mouth; the three hating ones: the liver, the gall, and the tongue; but God the faithful King, rules over all three systems. One (i. e., God) is over the three; the three are over the seven; the seven are over the twelve, and all are joined together, the one with the other" (VI, 3).

We also learn that the twenty-two letters, though a small number, by their power of "combination" and "transposition," yield an endless number of words and figures, and thus become the types of all the varied phenomena in the creation. "Just as the twenty-two letters yield two hundred and thirty-one types by combining Aleph (i. e., the first letter) with all the letters, and all the letters with Beth (i e., the second letter), so all the formations and all that is spoken proceed from one name" (ch. II, 4). To illustrate how these different types are obtained we will state that by counting the first letter with the second, the first letter with the third and so on with all the rest of the alphabet, we obtain 21 types; by combining the second letter with the third, fourth, etc., we get 20 types; the third letter combined with the fourth, etc., yields 19 types; finally the twenty-first combined with the last letter yields 1 type. In this way we get as the Hebrew table shows: $21+20+19+18+17+16+15+14+13+12+11+10+9+8+7+6+5+4+3+2+1=231$; or

ab ag ad ah av az a^{c}h at ai ak al am an as etc.

bg bd bh bv bz b^{c}h bt bi bk bl bm bn bs etc.

gd gh gv gz g^{c}h gt gi gk gl gm gn gs etc.

dh dv dz d^{c}h dt di dk dl dm dn ds etc.

hv hz h^{c}h ht hi hk hl hm hn hs etc.

The infinite variety in creation is still more strikingly exhibited by permutations, of which the Hebrew alphabet is capable, and through which an infinite variety of types is obtained. Hence the remark: "Two letters form two houses, three letters build six houses, four build twenty-four, five build a hundred and twenty houses, six build seven hundred and twenty houses;[19] and from thenceforward go out and think what the mouth cannot utter and the ear cannot hear" (IV, 4). A few examples may serve as illustration. Two letters form two houses, by using the first two letters of the Hebrew alphabet, a b,[20] in the following manner:

$$1 = ab$$
$$2 = ba$$

Three letters, a, b, g,[21] build six houses, namely:

$$1 = abg; \quad 2 = agb; \quad 3 = bag; \quad 4 = bga;$$
$$5 = gab; \quad 6 = gba.$$

Four letters, a, b, g, d,[22] build twenty-four houses, viz.:

$1 = abgd$	$13 = gabd$
$2 = abdg$	$14 = gadb$
$3 = agbd$	$15 = gbad$
$4 = agdb$	$16 = gbda$
$5 = adbg$	$17 = gdab$
$6 = adgb$	$18 = gdba$
$7 = bagd$	$19 = dabg$
$8 = badg$	$20 = dagb$
$9 = bgad$	$21 = dbag$

[19] In order to ascertain how often a certain number of letters can be transposed, the product of the preceding number must be multiplied with it, thus:

Letter $2 \times 1 =$	2	$5 \times$	$24 =$	120
$3 \times 2 =$	6	$6 \times$	$120 =$	720
$4 \times 6 =$	24	$7 \times$	$720 =$	5040 and so on.

[20] א ב
[21] א ב ג
[22] א ב ג ד

31

$$10 = bgda \qquad 22 = dbga$$
$$11 = bdag \qquad 23 = dgab$$
$$12 = bdga \qquad 24 = dgba$$

The Book of Creation closes with the statement: "And when Abraham our father had beheld, and considered, and seen, and drawn, and hewn, and obtained it, then the Lord of all revealed Himself to him, and called him His friend, and made a covenant with him and with his seed; and he believed in Jehovah, and it was computed to him for righteousness. He made with him a covenant between the ten toes, and that is circumcision; between the ten fingers of his hand, and that is the tongue; and He bound two-and-twenty letters on his tongue, and showed him their foundation. He drew them with water, He kindled them with fire, He breathed them with wind (air); He burnt them in seven; He poured them forth in the twelve constellations" (ch. VI, 4).

Romantic Cosmology.—The examination of the contents of the Book of Jezirah proves that it has as yet nothing in common with the cardinal doctrines of the Cabala, as exhibited in later works, especially in the Zohar, where speculations about the being and nature of the Deity, the En Soph[23] and the Sephiroth, which are the essence of the Cabala, are given.

To the period of the Book of Jezirah belongs the remarkable work which in the Amsterdam edition of 1601 is entitled: "This is the book of the first man, which was given to him by the angel Raziel." In this work the angel Raziel appears as the bearer and mediator of astrological and astronomical secrets, and shows the influence of the planets upon the sublunary world. To the same period belongs the Midrash Konen, a kind of romantic cosmology (newly translated into German by Wünsche in *Israels Lehrhallen,* III, Leipsic, 1909, pp. 170-201).

With the thirteenth century begins the crystallization of the Cabala, and Isaac the Blind (flourished 1190-1210) may be regarded as the originator of this lore. The doctrines of the Sephiroth[24] taught in the Book Jezirah are further developed by his pupils, especially by Rabbi Azariel (died 1238), in his "Commentary on the Ten Sephiroth, by Way of Questions and Answers," an analysis of which is given in Jellinek's *Beiträge zur Geschichte der Kabbalah,* Leipsic, 1852, Part II, p. 32 f. In this comment-

---

[23] *En Soph,* אֵין סוֹף = ἄπειρος, i. e., "Endless," "Boundless," is the name of the Deity given in the Zohar, where it is said of God (III, 283*b*) that he cannot be comprehended by the intellect, nor described in words, for there is nothing which can grasp and depict him to us, and as such he is, in a certain sense, not existent (אֵין).

[24] See above.

ary Azariel lays down the following propositions:

1. The primary cause and governor of the world is the En Soph (i. e., a being infinite, boundless), who is both immanent and transcendent.

2. From the En Soph emanated the Sephiroth which are the medium between the absolute En Soph and the real world.

3. There are ten intermediate Sephiroth.

4. They are emanations and not creations.

5. They are both active and passive.

6. The first Sephirah is called "Inscrutable Height" (*rum maalah*): the second, "Wisdom" (*chokma*); the third, "Intelligence" (*binah*); the fourth, "Love" (*chesed*); the fifth, "Justice" (*pachad*); the sixth, "Beauty" (*tipheret*); the seventh, "Firmness" (*nezach*); the eighth, "Splendor" (*hod*); the ninth, "the Righteous in the Foundation of the World" (*zadik yesod olam*); and the tenth, "Righteousness" (*zedaka*).

The first three Sephiroth form the world of thought; the second three the world of the soul; and the four last the world of body—thus corresponding to the intellectual, moral and natural worlds.

That Isaac the Blind must be regarded as "the Father of the Cabala," is acknowledged by some of the earliest and most intelligent Cabalists themselves. And the author of the cabalistic work entitled *Maarecheth haelohuth*, said to be a certain Perez of the second part of the thirteenth century, frankly declares that "the doctrine of the En Soph and the Ten Sephiroth is neither to be found in the Law, Prophets, or Hagiographa, nor in the writings of the Rabbins of blessed memory, but rests solely upon signs which are scarcely perceptible."

Another remarkable book of this period is the *Sepher Bahir*, or Midrash of Nehunjah ben-ha-Kanah. According to this work, long before the creation God caused a metaphysical matter to proceed, which became a fulness (*melo*) of blessing and salvation for all forms of existence. The ten divine emanations, which are not yet called Sephiroth, but *Maamarim* and appear as categories endowed with creative power, are connected with the attributes (*middoth*) of God as well as with his fingers and other members.

The doctrine of metempsychosis is already given here in its most important features. The work itself, though ascribed to Nehunjah is of much later date, because it speaks of the Hebrew vowels and accents. Only a part of the Bahir book has been published, first at Amsterdam, 1651; then again at Berlin, 1706. The greater part is still in manuscript in the libraries at Paris and Leyden.

The conversion of the famous Talmudist and scholar Moses Nachmanides[25] (1194-1270) to the newly-born Cabala gave to it an extraordinary importance and rapid spread amongst his numerous followers. In the division of the synagogues caused by the writings of Maimonides, Nachmanides took the part of the latter, probably more on account of the esteem he felt for this great man than for any sympathy with his opinions. Maimonides intended to give Judaism a character of unity, but he produced the contrary. His aim was to harmonize philosophy and religion, but the result was a schism in the synagogue, which gave birth to this queer kind of philosophy called Cabala, and to this newly-born Cabala Nachmanides became converted, though he was at first decidedly adverse to this system.

One day the Cabalist who was most zealous to convert him was caught in a house of ill-fame, and condemned to death. He requested Nachmanides to visit him on the Sabbath, the day fixed for his execution. Nachmanides reproved him for his sins, but the Cabalist declared his innocence, and that he would partake with him of the Sabbath meal. According to the story, he did as he promised, as by means of the Cabalistic mysteries he effected his escape, and an ass was

[25] See my article s. v. "Nachmanides" in McClintock and Strong's Cyclop.

executed in his stead, and he himself was suddenly transported into Nachmanides's house! From that time Nachmanides became a disciple of the Cabala, and was initiated into its mysteries, the tenets of which pervade his numerous writings, especially his commentary on the Pentateuch.

To the first half of the twelfth century belongs the *Massecheth Aziluth* or "the Treatise on the Emanations," supposed to have been written by Rabbi Isaac Nasir. From the analysis given by Jellinek (*Auswahl kabbalistischer Mystik,* Part I, Leipsic, 1853) we learn that the prophet Elijah propounded that

1. "God at first created light and darkness, the one for the pious and the other for the wicked, darkness having come to pass by the divine limitation of light.

2. "God produced and destroyed sundry worlds, which, like ten trees planted upon a narrow space, contend about the sap of the soil, and finally perish altogether.

3. "God manifested himself in four worlds, viz., Azila, Beriah, Jezirah and Asiah, corresponding to the four letters of his name J H V H. In the Azilatic luminous world is the divine Majesty, the Shechinah. In the Beriatic world are the souls of the pious, all the blessings, the throne of God, who sits on it in the form of Achteriël

(the crown of God, the first *Sephira Keter*), and the seven different luminous and splendid regions. In the Jeziratic world are the sacred animals in the vision of Ezekiel, the ten classes of angels with their princes, who are presided over by the fiery Metatron,[26] the spirits of men, and the accessory work of the divine chariot. In the Asilatic world are the Ophanim, the angels who receive the prayers, who are appointed over the will of man, who control the action of mortals, who carry on the struggle against evil, and who are presided over by the angelic prince Synadelphon.[27]

4. "The world was founded in wisdom and understanding (Prov. iii. 13), and God in his knowledge originated fifty gates of understanding.

5. "God created the world—as the book Jezirah already teaches—by means of the ten Sephiroth, which are both the agencies and qualities

---

[26] The angel who stands behind the throne of God.

[27] This Synadelphon is no doubt the same as "Sandalphon," the theme of Longfellow's poem of that name, which commences thus:

"Have you read in the Talmud of old,
In the Legends the Rabbins have told
Of the limitless realms of the air,
Have you read it,—the marvelous story
Of Sandalphon, the Angel of Glory,
Sandalphon, the Angel of Prayer?"

In a note on page 668 (Boston and New York edition, 1893) it is stated that Longfellow marked certain passages in Stehelin's *The Traditions of the Jews,* which evidently furnished the material.

of the Deity. The ten Sephiroth are called Crown, Wisdom, Intelligence, Mercy, Fear, Beauty, Victory, Majesty and Kingdom; they are merely ideal and stand above the concrete world" (pp. 2, 3).

The conversion of Todros ben Joseph Halevi Abulafia (1234-1304) to the Cabala, gave to this science a great influence, on account of Abulafia's distinguished position as physician and financier in the court of Sancho IV, King of Castile. The influence of Abulafia, whose works are still in manuscript, can be best seen from the fact that four Cabalists of the first rank ranged themselves under his banner and dedicated their compositions to him. These four Cabalists were Isaac Ibn Latif or Allatif, Abraham Abulafia, Joseph Gikatilla, and Moses de Leon, all Spaniards.

Mysteries of the Cabala.—Isaac Ibn Latif (about 1220-1290), starting with the thought that a philosophical view of Judaism was not the "right road to the sanctuary," endeavored to combine philosophy with Cabala. "He laid more stress than his predecessors on the close connection between the spiritual and the material world—between God and his creation. For the Godhead is in all, and all is in it. In soul-inspiring prayers the human spirit is raised to the world-spirit (*sechel ha-poel*), to which it is united 'in a kiss,' and, so influencing the Deity, it draws down blessings on the sublunar world. But not every mortal is capable of such spiritual and efficacious prayer; therefore the prophets, the most perfect men, were obliged to pray for the people, for they alone knew the power of prayer. The unfolding and revelation of the Deity in the world of spirits, spheres and bodies Allatif explained by mathematical forms. The mutual relation thereof is the same as "that of the point extending and thickening into a line, the line into the plane, the plane into the expanded body."

An enthusiastic contemporary of Allatif was Abraham ben Samuel Abulafia[28] (born at Saragossa, 1240; died 1291). He was an eccentric personage, full of whims, and fond of adventures. Not satisfied with philosophy, he gave himself to the mysteries of the Cabala in their most fantastic extremes, as the ordinary doctrine of the Sephiroth did not satisfy him. He sought after something higher, for prophetic inspiration. Through it he discovered a higher Cabala, which offered the means of coming into spiritual communion with the Godhead, and of obtaining prophetic insight. To analyze the words of Holy Writ,

[28] See my article *s. v.* "Abulafia" (*loc. cit.*, Vol. XI, p. 18) ; comp. also Günzburg, *Der Pseudo-Messias Abraham Abulafia, sein Leben und sein Wirken,* Cracow, 1904.

especially those of the divine name, to use the letters as independent notions (*Notaricon*), or to transpose the component parts of a word in all possible permutations, so as to form words from them (*Tsiruf*), or finally to employ the letters as numbers (*Gematria*), are indeed means of securing communion with the spirit-world; but this alone is not sufficient. To be worthy of a prophetic revelation, one must lead an ascetic life, retire into a quiet closet, banish all earthly cares, clothe himself in white garments, wrap himself up with *Talith* (i. e., the fringed garment) and Phylacteries, and devoutly prepare his soul, as if for an interview with the Deity. He must pronounce the letters of God's name at intervals, with modulations of the voice, or write them down in a certain order under divers energetic movements, turnings and bendings of the body, till the mind becomes dazed and the heart is filled with a glow. When one has gone through these practices and is in such a condition, the fulness of the Godhead is shed abroad in the human soul: the soul then unites itself with the divine soul in a kiss, and prophetic revelation follows quite naturally. In this way he laid down his Cabala, in antithesis to the superficial or baser Cabala, which occupies itself with the Sephiroth, and, as he gibingly said, erects a sort of "ten unity" instead of the Christian Trinity.

Abulafia went to Italy, and in Urbino he published (1279) prophetic writings, in which he records his conversations with God. In 1281 he undertook to convert the Pope, Martin IV, to Judaism. In Messina he imagined that it was revealed to him that he was the Messiah, and announced that the restoration of Israel would take place in 1296. Many believed in him and prepared themselves for returning to the holy land. Others, however, raised such a storm of opposition that Abulafia had to escape to the island of Comino, near Malta (about 1288), where he remained for some time, and wrote sundry Cabalistic works. Of his many works Jellinek published his Rejoinder to Solomon ben Adereth, who attacked his doctrines and pretensions as Messiah and prophet.

A disciple of Abulafia was *Joseph Gikatilla* of Medina-Celi, who died in Penjafiel after 1305. He, too, occupied himself with the mysticism of letters and numbers, and with the transposition of letters. His writings are in reality only an echo of Abulafia's fancies: the same delusion is apparent in both. Gikatilla's system is laid down in his *Ginnath egos,* i. e., "Garden of Nuts," published at Hanau, 1615; and *Shaare ora,* i. e., "the Gate of Light," first published at Mantua, 1561,

---

[29] *Auswahl kabbalistischer Mystic,* Part I, pp. 20-25 (German part).

in Cracow, 1600, and translated into Latin by Knorr von Rosenroth in the first part of his *Kabbala Denudata*, Sulzbach, 1677-78.

But far more influential and more pernicious than Allatif, Abulafia and Gikatilla was Moses de Leon (born in Leon about 1250, died in Arevalo, 1305), the author of a book which gave the Cabala a firm foundation and wide circulation,— in brief, raised it to the zenith of its power. This book is known by the name of Zohar or Splendor. At first he published his productions under his own name (about 1285). But as his writings were not sufficiently noticed, and brought him but little fame and money, he hit upon a much more effective means and commenced the composition of books under feigned but honored names. If he put the doctrines of the Cabala into the mouth of an older, highly venerated authority, he was sure to be successful in every respect. And he selected for this purpose the Tanaite Simon ben Jochaï,[30] who according to tradition spent thirteen years in a cave, solitary and buried in profound reflection, and whom ancient mysticism represented as receiving revelations from the prophet Elijah. Simon ben Jochaï was assuredly the right authority for the Cabala. But he must not write or speak Hebrew, but Chaldee, a language peculiarly fit for secrets, and

[30] See my article *s. v.* in McClintock and Strong's *Cyclop.*, Vol. IX, p. 757.

sounding as if from another world. And thus there came into the world a book, the "Zohar," which for many centuries was held by the Jews as a heavenly revelation, and was studied even by Christians.

CHAPTER III.

THE ZOHAR.

The Book of Splendor.—The titles of the Zohar vary. It is called "Midrash of Rabbi Simon ben Jochaï," from its reputed author: "Midrash, Let there be Light," from the words in Gen. i. 4; more commonly *"Sepher ha-Zohar,"* from Dan. xii. 3, where the word *Zohar* is used for "the brightness of the firmament." The title in full is: *Sepher ha-Zohar al ha-Torah, me-ish Elohim Kodesh, hu more meod ha-tana R. Simon ben Jochaï,* etc., i. e., "The Book of Splendor on the Law, by the very holy and venerable man of God, the Tanaite rabbi Simon ben Jochaï, of blessed memory."

The *editio princeps* is the one of Mantua (3 vols., 1558-1560) and has often been reprinted. The best edition of the book of Zohar is that by Christian Knorr von Rosenroth, with Jewish commentaries (Sulzbach, 1684, fol.) to which his rare *Kabbala Denudata* (1677-1684) forms an ample introduction. This edition was reprinted with an additional index (Amsterdam, 1714, 1728, 1772, 1805, 3 vols.). Recent editions of the Zohar were published at Breslau (1866, 3 vols.), Livorno (1877-78, in 7 parts), and Wilna (1882, 3 vols.; 1882-83 in 10 parts, containing many commentaries and additions).

The body of the work takes the form of a commentary of a highly mystic and allegorical character extending over the entire Pentateuch; but the Zohar is not considered complete without the addition of certain appendices attributed to the same author or to some of his personal or successional disciples.

These supplementary portions are:

1. *Siphra di Tseniutha,* i. e., "The Book of Secrets" or "Mysteries," contained in Vol. II, 176-178. It contains five chapters and is chiefly occupied with discussing the questions involved in the creation. In the second and third chapters the prophet Elijah communicates the secret which he learned in the heavenly school, that before the creation of the world God was unknown to man, but made known his essence after the creation of the world. The history of the creation is represented under the figure of a scale, which adjusts the opposite aspects of God before and after the creation. This portion has been translated into Latin by Rosenroth in the second volume of his *Kabbala Denudata* (Frankfort-on-

the-Main, 1684; Englished by Mathers, *loc, cit.,* pp. 43-108).

2. *Iddera Rabba,* i. e., "The Great Assembly," referring to the community or college of Simon's disciples in their conferences for cabalistic discussion. These discussions are chiefly occupied with a description of the form and various members of the Deity; a disquisition on the revelation of the Deity, in his two aspects of the "Aged" and the "Young," to the creation and the universe; as well as on the diverse gigantic members of the Deity, such as the head, the beard, the eyes, the nose, etc., etc.; a dissertion on pneumatology, demonology, etc., etc. This part is generally found in Vol. III, pp. 127*b*-145*a,* and has been translated into Latin by Rosenroth, *loc. cit,* and Englished by Mathers, pp. 109-257.

3. *Iddera Zuta,* i. e., "The Small Assembly," referring to the few disciples who still assembled for cabalistic discussion towards the end of their master's life or after his decease. It is to a great extent a recapitulation of the *Iddera Rabba,* and concludes with recording the death of Simon ben Jochaï, the Sacred Light and the medium through whom God revealed the contents of the Zohar. This part is found in Vol. III, 287*b*-296*b,* and from the Latin of Rosenroth (Vol. II of the *Kabbala Denudata*) it has been Englished by Mathers, pp. 259-341.

To these three larger appendices are added fifteen other minor fragments, viz.:

4. *Saba,* i. e., "The Aged Man," also called
"Saba demishpatim," or "The Discourse of the
Aged in Mishpatim," given in II, 94a-114a. "The
Aged" is the prophet Elijah who holds converse
with Rabbi Simon about the doctrine of metem-
psychosis, and the discussion is attached to the
Sabbatic section called "Mishpatim," i. e., Exod.
xxi, 1-xxiv. 18.

5. Midrash Ruth, a fragment.

6. *Sepher hab-bahir,* i. e., "The Book of Clear
Light."

7 and 8. *Tosephta* and *Mattanitan,* i. e., "Small
Additional Pieces," which are found in the three
volumes.

9. *Raïa mehemna,* i. e., "The Faithful Shepherd," found in the second and third volumes.
The faithful shepherd is Moses who holds a dialogue with Rabbi Simon, at which not only the
prophet Elijah is present, but Abraham, Isaac,
Jacob, Aaron, David, Solomon, and even God
himself make their appearance.

10. *Hekaloth,* i. e., "The palaces," found in
the first and second volumes, treats of the topo-
graphical structure of paradise and hell.

11. *Sithre Torah,* i. e., "The Secrets of the
Law."

12. *Midrash han-neelam,* i. e., "The Concealed

"Treatise," in which passages of Scripture are explained mystically. Thus Lot's two daughters are the two proclivities in man, good and evil (I, 110). It also discourses on the properties and destiny of the soul.

13. *Raze de Razin*, i. e., "Mysteries of Mysteries," contained in II, *70a-75a*, is especially devoted to the physiognomy of the Cabala, and the connection of the soul with the body.

14. *Midrash Chazith*, on the Song of Songs.

15. *Maamar to Chazi*, a discourse, so entitled from the first words, "Come and see."

16. *Yanuka*, i. e., "The Youth," given in III, *186a-192a*, records the discourses delivered by a young man who according to R. Simon was of superhuman origin.

17. *Pekuda*, i. e., "Illustrations of the Law."

18. *Chibbura Kadmaah*, i. e., "The Early Work."

The body of the work is sometimes called *Zohar Gadol*, "The Great Zohar."

Authorship of the Zohar.—Who is the author of this remarkable book, which has continued to be a text-book up to the present day, for all those who have espoused the doctrines of the Cabala? We have anticipated the answer, but let us see which reasons were adduced by modern scholarship to prove that the Zohar is a forgery of the thirteenth century.

Now the Zohar pretends to be a revelation from God communicated through Rabbi Simon ben Jochaï to his select disciples, according to the Iddera Zuta (Zohar III, 287*b*). This declaration and the repeated representation of Rabbi Simon ben Jochaï, as speaking and teaching throughout the production fixed the authorship upon Rabbi Simon, an opinion maintained not only by Jews for centuries, but even by distinguished Christian scholars. On the other hand it has been clearly demonstrated by such Jewish scholars as Zunz, Geiger, Jellinek, Graetz, Steinschneider, and a host of others, that the Zohar is not the production of Rabbi Simon, but of the thirteenth century, by Moses de Leon (1250-1305).[1] Simon ben Jochaï was a pupil of Rabbi Akiba; but the earliest mention of the book's existence occurs in the year 1290, and the anachronisms of its style and in the facts referred to, together with the circumstance that it speaks of the vowel-points and other Masoretic inventions which are clearly

---

[1] See my article *s. v.* in McClintock and Strong. Professor Strack, who is entitled to a hearing in matters of Rabbinic literature, says: "He [Rabbi Simon] has long been regarded as the author of the Zohar; but this main work of the Cabala was in reality composed in Spain by Moses ben Shem Tob de Leon in the second half of the thirteenth century, as has been proved especially by Jacob Emden, in *Mitpahath Sepharim*, Altona, 1768."—*Einleitung in den Talmud*, 4th ed., Leipsic, 1908, p. 93.

posterior to the Talmud, justify J. Morinus (although too often extravagant in his wilful attempts to depreciate the antiquity of the latter Jewish writings) in asserting that the author could not have lived much before the year 1000 of the Christian era (*Exercitationes Biblicae*, pp. 358-369). This later view of the authorship is sustained by the following reasons:

1. The Zohar most fulsomely praises its own author, calls him the Sacred Light, and exalts him above Moses, "the faithful Shepherd" (Zohar III, 132*b*; 144*a*), while the disciples deify Rabbi Simon, before whom all men must appear (II, 38*a*).

2. The Zohar quotes and mystically explains the Hebrew vowel-points (I, 16*b*, 24*b*; II, 116*a*; III, 65*a*), which were introduced later.[2]

3. The Zohar (II, 32*a*) mentions the Crusades, the temporary taking of Jerusalem by the Crusaders from the Infidels, and the retaking of it by the Saracens.

4. The Zohar (III, 212*b*) records events which transpired A. D. 1264.

5. The doctrine of *En-Soph* and the *Sephiroth*, as well as the metempsychosian retribution, were not known before the thirteenth century.

6. The very existence of the Zohar, according to the stanch Cabalist Jehudah Chayoth (about

[2] See my article "Vowel-Points" in McClintock and Strong.

1500), was unknown to such distinguished Cabalists as Nachmanides and Ben-Adereth (1235-1310); the first who mentions it is Todros Abulafia (1234-1306).

7. Isaac of Akko (about 1290) affirms that "The Zohar was put into the world from the head of a Spaniard."

8. The Zohar contains passages which Moses de Leon translated into Aramaic from his works, e. g., the *Sepher ha-Rimmon,* as Jellinek has demonstrated in his *Moses de Leon und sein Verhältniss zum Sohar,"* Leipsic, 1851, p. 21-36; (see also Graetz, *Geschichte der Juden,* VII, 498; 2d ed., 1873, p. 477 et seq.).

These are some of the reasons why the Zohar is now regarded as a pseudograph of the thirteenth century, and that Moses de Leon should have palmed the Zohar upon Simon ben Jochaï was nothing remarkable, since this rabbi is regarded by tradition as the embodiment of mysticism. There was also a financial reason, for from the Book *Juchasin* (pp. 88, 89, 95, ed. Filipowski, London, 1857) we learn that when his wife asked him why he published the production of his own intellect under another man's name, Moses de Leon replied "that if he were to publish it under his own name nobody would buy it, whereas under the name of Rabbi Simon ben Jochaï it yielded him a large revenue."

With the appearance of the Zohar we find also a Zohar School, which is a combination and absorption of the different features and doctrines of all the former methods, without any plan or method; and we must not be surprised at the wild speculations which we so often find in the writings of the post-Zohar period. In Spain especially the study of the Zohar took deep root, and found its way to Italy, Palestine and Poland.

CHAPTER IV.

THE CABALA IN THE POST-ZOHAR PERIOD.

Visionary Teachings.—The new text-book of religion which was introduced into Judaism by stealth, "placed the Kabbala, which a century before had been unknown, on the same level as the Bible and the Talmud, and to a certain extent on a still higher level. The Zohar undoubtedly produced good, in so far as it opposed enthusiasm to the legal dry-as-dust manner of the study of the Talmud, stimulated the imagination and the feelings, and cultivated a disposition that restrained the reasoning faculty. But the ills which it has brought on Judaism outweigh the good by far. The Zohar confirmed and propagated a gloomy superstition, and strengthened in people's minds the belief in the Kingdom of Satan, in evil spirits and ghosts. Through its constant use of coarse expression, often verging on the sensual, in contradistinction to the chaste, pure spirit pervading Jewish literature, the Zohar sowed the seeds of unclean desires, and later on produced a sect that laid aside all regard for decency. Finally, the Zohar blunted the sense for the simple and the true, and created a visionary world in which the souls of those who zealously occupied themselves with it were lulled into a sort of half-sleep and lost the faculty of distinguishing between right and wrong. Its quibbling interpretations of Holy Writ, adopted by the Kabbalists and others infected with this mannerism, perverted the verses and words of the Holy Book, and made the Bible the wrestling-ground of the most curious insane notions."

During the thirteenth century the Cabala was represented in Italy by Menahem di Recanati who wrote a commentary on the Pentateuch which is little else than a commentary on the Zohar. This work was translated into Latin by Pico della Mirandola.

At the beginning of the fourteenth century Joseph ben Abraham ibn Wakkar (1290-1340) endeavored to reconcile the Cabala with philosophy, and to this end wrote a treatise on the cardinal doctrines of the Cabala. An analysis of this treatise, which is still in manuscript in the Bodleian library (cod. Laud. 119; described by Uri No. 384) is given by Steinschneider in Ersch und Gruber's *Allgemeine Encyclopädie*, Part II, Vol. XXXI, p. 100 f.

During the fourteenth and fifteenth centuries
the Cabala was especially cultivated in Spain. In
unmeasured terms the Zoharites denounced their
co-religionists who could not see the advantages
of the Cabala. Prominent among the Zoharites
was Abraham of Granada, who composed (between 1391 and 1409) a cabalistic work *Berith
menuchat,* "The Covenant of Peace," (Amsterdam, 1648), a farrago of strange names of the
Deity and the angels, of transposed letters, and
jugglery with vowels and accents. "He had the
hardihood," says Graetz, "to teach that those who
could not apprehend God by Cabalistic methods
belonged to the weak in faith, were ignorant sinners, and like the depraved and the apostate were
overlooked by God, and not found worthy of
His special providence. He thought that the re-
linquishment of their religion by cultured Jews
was explained by their fatal application to scientific study, and their contempt for the Cabala.
On the other hand he professed to see in the per-
secutions of 1391, and in the conversion of so
many prominent Jews to Christianity, the tokens
of the Messianic age, the suffering that must pre-
cede it, and the approach of the redemption."
Another such writer was Shem Tob ben Joseph
ibn Shem Tob (died 1430), author of *Emunoth,*
i. e., "Faithfulness" (Ferrara, 1557), in which
he attacks Jewish thinkers and philosophers as

heretics, and maintains that the salvation of Israel depends upon the Cabala. The third writer was Moses Botarel (or Botarelo), also a Spaniard, who claimed to be a thaumaturge and prophet, and even announced himself as the Messiah. He prophesied that in the spring of 1393 the Messianic age would be ushered in. As the Cabala penetrated all branches of life and literature, voices were also raised against the Zohar. The first among the Jews who opposed its authority was Elias del Medigo, who in his *Bechinath ha-daath* (i. e., "Examination of the Law," written in December, 1491) openly expressed his opinion that the Zohar was the production of a forger, and that the Cabala was made up of the rags and tatters of the neo-Platonic school. But his voice and that of others had no power to check the rapid progress of the Cabala, which had now found its way from Spain and Italy into Palestine and Poland.

Wonder Workers and Prophets.—Passing over some minor advocates and teachers of the Cabala, we must mention two scholars in Palestine, who distinguished themselves as masters of the Cabala, Moses Cordovero[1] and Isaac Luria. The former (1522-1570) was a pupil of Solomon Alkabez[2] and wrote many works on the Cabala. His principal work is the *Pardes Rim-monim*, i.

[1] See my article *s. v.* "Moses Cordovero," *loc. cit.*

e., "The Garden of Pomegranates." (Cracow, 1591), excerpts of which have been translated into Latin by Bartolocci in *Bibliotheca Magna Rabbinicia,* Vol. IV, p. 231 f., and by Knorr von Rosenroth, *"Tractatus de Anima ex libro Pardes Rimonim"* in his *Kabbala Denudata,* Sulzbach, 1677. Cordovero is chiefly occupied with the scientific speculations of the Cabala, or the speculative Cabala, in contradistinction to the wonder-working Cabala, which was represented by Isaac Luria (born in Jerusalem in 1534, and died 1572). He claimed to have constant interviews with the prophet Elijah, who communicated to him sublime doctrines. He visited the sepulchers of ancient teachers, and there, by prostrations and prayers, obtained from their spirits all manner of revelations. He was convinced that he was the Messiah, the son of Joseph, and that he was able to perform all sorts of miracles. He imagined a complete system of transmigration and combination of souls. He saw spirits everywhere; he saw how the souls were set free from the body at death, how they hovered in the air, or rose out of their graves. On the Sabbath he dressed in white, and wore a fourfold garment to symbolize the four letters of the name of God. His sentiments he delivered orally and his disciples treas-

---

[2] He is the author of a hymn *"Lecha dodi,"* i. e., "Come my beloved," which is found in all Jewish prayer-books, and used in the service for Sabbath eve.

ured up his marvelous sayings, whereby they performed miracles and converted thousands to the doctrines of this theosophy.

His disciples were divided into two classes, the "initiated" and the "novices," who boastfully called themselves *"guré ari,"* i. e., "the lion's whelps." They systematically circulated the most absurd stories about Luria's miracles, and thus it came about that his cabalistic doctrines caused inexpressible harm in Jewish circles. Through Luria's influence a Judaism of the Zohar and the Cabala was formed side by side with the Judaism of the Talmud and the rabbis; for it was due to him that the spurious Zohar was placed upon a level with, indeed higher than, the Holy Scriptures and the Talmud.

The real exponent of Luria's cabalistic system was Chayim Vital Calabrese[3] (1543-1620). After his master's death he diligently collected all the manuscript notes of the lectures delivered by Luria, which together with his own jottings Vital published under the title of *Ez chayim,* i. e., "The Tree of Life,"[4] having spent over thirty years upon their preparation. The work consists of six parts; that portion which treats of the doctrine of metempsychosis (*Hagilgulim*), is found

[3] See my article *s. v.* "Vital" in McClintock and Strong.

[4] For a description of the component parts of this work, see Fürst, *Bibliotheca Judaica,* III, pp. 479-481.

in a Latin translation in Knorr von Rosenroth's work.

The Luria-Vital system found many adherents everywhere. Abraham de Herera (died 1639) wrote in Spanish two cabalistic works, the "House of God" (*beth Elohim*) and the "Gate of Heaven" (*shaar ha-shemayim*), which the Amsterdam preacher Isaac Aboab translated into Hebrew. Both are given in a Latin translation in Knorr von Rosenroth's work, together with a translation of "The Valley of the King" (*emek ha-melech*) by Naphtali Frankfurter. Besides these we may mention Isaiah Horwitz (died at Tiberias in 1629), author of *Sh'ne luchoth haberith* (abbreviated *Shela*), i. e., "The Two Tables of the Covenant," a kind of Real-Encyclopedia of Judaism on a cabalistic basis. This work has been often reprinted and enjoys a great reputation among the Jews. Abridgments of it were frequently published (Amsterdam, 1683; Venice, 1705; Warsaw, 1879).

There were not wanting those who opposed the Cabala. Of the numerous opponents which the Zohar and Luria-Vital's works called forth, none was so daring, so outspoken and powerful as Leon de Modena of Venice (1571-1648). He is best known as the author of *Historia dei Riti Hebraici ed observanza degli Hebrei di questi tempi*, or the "History of the Rites, Customs and

Manner of Life of the Jews" (Padua, 1640), and translated into Latin, French, Dutch, English.[5] But besides this and other works, he also wrote a polemical treatise against the Cabalists, whom he despised and derided, entitled *Ari noham,* i. e., "Roaring Lion," published by Julius Fürst, Leipsic, 1840. In this treatise he shows that the cabalistic works, "which are palmed upon ancient authorities, are pseudonymous; that the doctrines themselves are mischievous; and that the followers of this system are inflated with proud notions, pretending to know the nature of God better than any one else, and to possess the nearest and best way of approaching the Deity." He even went so far as to question whether God will ever forgive those who printed the cabalistic works (comp. Fürst, p. 7), and this no doubt, because so many Cabalists joined the Church.

But no opposition could stem the tide of the Cabala. Its wonder-working branch had now largely laid hold on the minds and fancies of the Jews, and was producing among them the most mournful and calamitous effects. The chief actor in this tragedy was the cabalist Sabbatai Zebi,[6]

[5] The English translation is found in Picard's *Ceremonies and Religious Customs of the Various Nations of the Known World,* Vol. I, London, 1733.

[6] See my article *s. v.* "Sabbatai Zebi" in McClintock and Strong; see also *Geschichte des Sabbatai-Zebi, sein Leben und Treiben,* Warsaw, 1883; and *Der Erzbetrüger Sabbatai Sevi, der letzte falsche Messias der Juden,* etc., Halle, 1760; Berlin, 1908.

born at Smyrna, July, 1641. When fifteen years
of age he rapidly mastered the mysteries of the
Cabala, which he expounded before crowded aud-
iences at the age of eighteen. When twenty-four
years of age, he revealed to his disciples that he
was the Messiah, the son of David, the true Re-
deemer, and that he was to redeem and deliver
Israel from their captivity. At the same time he
publicly pronounced the Tetragrammaton,[7] which
the high priest was only permitted to do on the
day of atonement. As he would not desist, he
was excommunicated by the Jewish sages at
Smyrna. He went to Salonica, Athens, Morea
and Jerusalem, teaching his doctrines, proclaim-
ing himself the Messiah, anointing prophets and
converting thousands upon thousands. As his
followers prepared to be led back by him to Jerusalem, they wound up their affairs, and in many
places trade was entirely stopped. By the order
of the Sultan, Mohammed IV, Sabbathai Zevi
was arrested and taken before him at Adrian-
ople. The Sultan said to him: "I am going to
test thy Messiahship. Three poisoned arrows
shall be shot into thee, and if they do not kill
thee, I too will believe that thou art the Messiah."
He saved himself by embracing Islamism in the
presence of the Sultan, who gave him the name
Effendi, and appointed him Kapidji-Bashi. Sab-

[7] Called by the Jews *shem-hammephorash,* on which
see my article *s. v.* in McClintock and Strong.

bathai died Sept. 10, 1676, after having ruined thousands upon thousands of Jewish families. In spite of this fiasco the number of Sabbathai's followers was not diminished.

Famous as a champion of orthodoxy was Jacob Israel Emden (1696-1776) rabbi of Altona. During his rabbinate there, the famous Jonathan Eybenschütz[8] (born in Cracow in 1690) was called to Altona in 1750, since the German and Polish Jews were divided in that place. As every rabbi was regarded as a sort of magician, the new-comer was expected to stop the epidemic raging at that time in the city. Eybenschütz prepared amulets, which he distributed among the people. For curiosity's sake one was opened, and lo! in it was written: "O thou God of Israel, who dwellest in the beauty of thy power, send down salvation to this person through the merit of thy servant Sabbathai Zevi, in order that thy name, and the name of the Messiah Sabbathai Zevi, may be hallowed in the world." This amulet came into the hands of Emden. Eybenschütz denied all connection with the adherents of Sabbathai, and as he had already gained a great influence, he was believed; at least, almost everybody kept quiet. But Emden was not quiet, and finally the ban was pronounced against Eybenschütz. Even the King Frederic V of Den-

[8] See my article s. v. "Eybenschütz" in loc. cit., Vol. XII, p. 367.

mark sided with Emden, and Eybenschütz lost
his position. Being forsaken by his friends, Eybenschütz went to his former pupil, Moses Ger-
son Kohen, who after baptism took the name of
Karl Anton. Anton wrote an apology in behalf
of his teacher, which he dedicated to the King of
Denmark. This and other influences had the
effect that the whole affair was dropped and Eybenschütz was elected anew as rabbi of the con-
gregation. Eybenschütz died in 1764 and was
followed twelve years later by his opponent Emden. Both are buried in the Jewish cemetery of
Altona.

Another Zoharite was Jacob Frank[9] (Jankiew
Lebowicz), the founder of the Jewish sect of the
Frankists, born in Poland in 1712. He acquired
a great reputation as a Cabalist, and settled in
Podolia, where he preached a new doctrine, the
fundamental principles of which he had borrowed
from the teachings of Sabbathai Zevi. He was
arrested through the influence of the rabbis, but
was liberated through the intervention of the Ro-
man Catholic clergy, and authorized by the King
to profess freely his tenets. His followers then,
under the name of Zoharites and Anti-Talmud-
ists oppressed their former adversaries in turn.
As the papal nuncio at Warsaw declared against
them, Frank and most of his adherents embraced

[9] Comp. Graetz, *Frank und die Frankisten*, Berlin,
1868.

Christianity. Frank continued to make proselytes and his sect increased in Poland and Bohemia. He lived in princely style on means furnished him by his followers, and died at Offenbach, in Hesse, December 10, 1791.

The Cabalists of the eighteenth century, with the exception of Moses Chayim Luzzatto (born 1707, died 1747), are of little importance. Modern influences gradually put a stop to the authority of the Cabala, and modern Judaism sees in the Cabala in general only an historical curiosity or an object of literary historical disquisitions.

CHAPTER V.

THE MOST IMPORTANT DOCTRINES OF THE CABALA.

God and Creation.—After having become acquainted in previous chapters with the principal actors in the cabalistic drama we are now prepared to examine the tenets of the Cabala.

Different from the system as exhibited in the Book of Creation or Jezirah is that of the Zohar, because the more difficult, since it embraces not merely the origin of the world, but likewise speculates on the essence of God and the properties of man; in other words it treats of theology, cosmology and anthropology.

Starting from the idea of the Supreme Being as boundless in his nature—which necessarily implies that he is an absolute unity and inscrutable, and that there is nothing without him—God is called *En Soph,* i. e., "endless," "boundless." In this boundlessness God cannot be comprehended by the intellect, nor described in words; for there is nothing which can grasp him and depict him to us,[1] and as such he is in a certain sense not existent (*ayin*); since, as far as our mind is concerned, that which is incomprehensible does not exist.

The En Soph, not being an object of cognition, made his existence known in the creation of the world by means of attributes or mediums, the ten Sephiroth, or intelligences, radiations, emanations, emanating from the En Soph, and which in their totality represent and are called the *Adam Kadmon*, the "Primordial or Archetypal Man."

The first Sephirah is called *Kether*, "Crown"; the second *Chochma*, "Wisdom"; the third *Bina*, "Intelligence"; the fourth *Chesed*, "Mercy"; the fifth *Dîn*, "Judgment"; the sixth *Tiphereth*, "Beauty"; the seventh *Nezach*, "Splendor"; the eighth *Hôd*, "Majesty"; the ninth *Jesôd*, "Foundation"; the tenth *Malchûth*, "Kingdom."

Now the first Sephirah, which is called the Crown, the Aged,[2] the Primordial or the Smooth Point,[3] the White Head, the Long Face, *Macro-*

---

[1] Rabbi Azariel in his commentary on the ten Sephiroth tells us that "the En Soph can neither be comprehended by the intellect, nor described in words; for there is no letter or word which can grasp him." With this compare what Proclus, the neo-Platonist, says in his *Theology of Plato*, II, 6: "Although the Divinity is generally called the unity (τὸ ἕν) or the first, it would be better if no name were given him; for there is no word which can depict his nature—he is the inexpressible (ἄρρητος), the unknown (ἀγνωστός). Isaac ibn Latif (1220-1290) even says "God is in all, and everything is in God."

prosopon, the Inscrutable Height,[4] contained the other nine Sephiroth and gave rise to them in the following order: from the first Sephirah proceeded a masculine or active potency designated (2) *Chochma,* "Wisdom," and an opposite, i. e., a feminine or passive potency, called (3) *Bina,* "Intelligence." These two opposite potencies are joined together by the first potency, and thus yield the first triad of the Sephiroth. From the junction of the foregoing opposites, which are also called "Father" (*abba*) and "Mother" (*imma*) emanated again the masculine or active potency called (4) *Chesed,* "Mercy or Love," also *Gedulah,* "Greatness," and from this again emanated the feminine or passive potency called (5) *Din,* "Judgment," also *Geburah,* "Judical Power." From this again emanated the uniting potency (6) *Tiphereth,* "Beauty." We have thus the second trinity of the Sephiroth. Now Beauty beamed forth the masculine or active potency (7) *Nezach,* "Splendor," and this again gave rise to (8) the feminine or passive potency *Hod,* "Majesty"; from it again emanated (9) *Jesôd,* "Foun-

[2] This must not be confounded with "the Aged of the Aged" as the En Soph is called.

[3] When the Concealed of the Concealed wished to reveal himself, he first made a single point; the Infinite was entirely unknown, and diffused no light before this luminous point violently broke through into vision." (Zohar, I, 15*a*.)

[4] So called by Rabbi Azariel.

dation," which yields the third trinity. From *Jesôd*, finally emanated (10) *Malchûth*, "Kingdom," also called Schechinah.

The Cabalists delight in representing the ten Sephiroth under different forms; now as *Adam Kadmon*, "Primordial or Archetypal Man," now as the cabalistic tree or the *Ilân*, in which the crown is represented by the first Sephirah and the root by the last.

The Divine Man.—As to the Adam Kadmon which is shown in the following figure, the Crown represents the head; Wisdom, the brains; Intelligence which unites the two and produces the first triad, the heart or the understanding. The fourth and fifth Sephiroth, i. e., Love and Justice are the two arms, the former the right arm and the latter the left; one distributing life and the other death. The sixth Sephirah, Beauty, uniting these two opposites and producing the second triad, is the chest. Firmness and Splendor of the third triad represent the two legs, whereas Foundation, the ninth Sephirah, represents the genital organs, since it denotes the basis and source of all things. Finally Kingdom, the tenth Sephirah, represents the harmony of the whole Archetypal Man.

Now in looking at the Sephiroth which constitute the first triad, it will be seen that they

represent the intellect; hence this triad is called
by Azariel the "intellectual world" (*olam muskal*

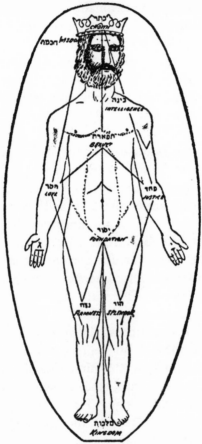

Fig. 1. ADAM KADMON, THE ARCHETYPAL MAN.

or *olam ha-sechel*). The second triad which represents moral qualities, is called the "moral" or "sensuous world" (*olam murgash,* also *olam ha-*

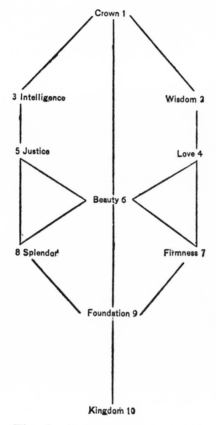

Fig. 2. THE CABALISTIC TREE.

nephesh) ; and the third, representing power and stability, is called the "material world" (*olam mutba* or *olam ha-teba*).

As concerns the cabalistic tree (the *ilân ha-ca-*

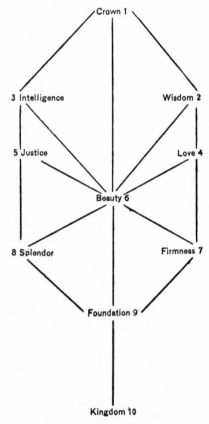

Fig. 3. THE PILLAR ARRANGEMENT.

bala), the Sephiroth are so arranged that the first triad is placed above, the second and third are

placed below, in such a manner that the three masculine Sephiroth are on the right, the three feminine on the left, whilst the four uniting Sephiroth occupy the center, as shown in Fig 2.

According to another arrangement the Sephiroth are so ordered that they form three pillars, a right one (*sitra dimina,* also *amuda de-chesed,* i. e., the pillar of mercy); a left one (*sitra dismola,* also *amuda de-dina,* i. e., the pillar of judgment), and a middle one (*amuda de-emzaïta*). In the right pillar to which belong the Sephiroth Wisdom, Love and Firmness, is life; in the left with the Sephiroth Intelligence, Judgment, Splendor, is Death. The middle pillar comprises Crown, Beauty, Foundation. The basis of all three pillars is the Kingdom. Fig. 3 illustrates this.

So far as the Sephiroth represent the first manifestation of God they form a world for themselves, an ideal world which has nothing to do with the real, material world. As such it is now called the primordial, the Archetypal Man (*Adam Kadmon*), now the Heavenly Man (*Adam Ilaî*). As for the Adam Kadmon, different views exist in the cabalistic writings. He is sometimes taken as the totality of the Sephiroth, and he appears as a pre-Sephirotic first emanation and superior to them, by which God manifested himself as creator and ruler of the

world, as it were a prototype (macrocosm) of
the entire creation. In this case it would seem as
if the Adam Kadmon were a first manifestation,
inserted between God and the world, so to say a
second God[5] or the divine Word.[6]

According to a later theorem four worlds proceed by an emanation in different gradations.
This is expressed by Ibn Latif thus: As the
point extends and thickens into a line, the line
into the plane, the plane into the expanded body,
thus God's self-manifestation unfolds itself in
the different worlds.

In each of these four worlds the ten Sephiroth
recur. The first Sephirah gave birth to the *Olam
azîla* or "world of emanation," containing the
powers of the divine plan of the world. Its beings have the same nature as that belonging to
the world of the Sephiroth or to the Adam Kadmon. This world which is also called the *olam
ha-sephiroth*, i. e., "the world of the Sephiroth,"
is the seat of the Shechinah. From the *olam
azîla* proceeded the *olam beria* or "world of creation," in which according to Rabbi Isaac Nasir[7]
are the souls of the saints, all the blessings, the

---

[5] δεύτερος θεὸς.

[6] λόγος.

[7] He flourished in the first half of the twelfth cen-
tury and is the author of a treatise on the Emanations
(*Massecheth Aziluth*) reprinted by Jellinek in his
Auswahl Kabbalistischer Mystik, Part I. Leipsic, 1853.

throne of the Deity, and the palaces of all spiritual and moral perfection. The *olam beria* gave birth to the *olam jezîrah* or "world of formation," in which dwell the holy angels, whose prince is Metatron.[8] But there are also the demons, which on account of their grossly sensual nature are called *Keliphoth,* "shells," and inhabit the planets and other heavenly bodies or the realm of the ether.

The fourth world is called *olam assiya,* the "world of action." Its substances consist of matter limited by space and perceptible to the senses in a multiplicity of forms. It is subject to constant changes, generations, and corruptions, and is the abode of the Evil Spirit.

Like the Talmud and the Midrash, the Zohar represents the optimistic view, that the present world is the best. Thus we read (Zohar, III, 292*b*: "There were old worlds, which perished as soon as they came into existence; they were formless, and were called sparks. Thus the smith

---

[8] Graetz, *Gnosticismus und Judentum,* 1846, p. 44, derives the word from μετὰ θρόνον, because this angel is immediately under the divine throne. Cassel (Ersch and Gruber's *Encyklopädie,* section II, vol. XXVII, s. v. "Juden," p .40, note 84) derives it from *metator,* i. e., "messenger, outrider, pathfinder." Wünsche also connects it with μετάτωρ. According to the Zohar, I, 126*b*, Metatron is the first creature of God; the middle pillar (in the essence of God) or the uniting link in the midst, comprising all grades, from top downwards, and from the bottom upwards (*ibid.,* III, 127*a*); the visibly manifested Deity (*ibid.,* III, 231*a*).

when hammering the iron, lets the sparks fly in all directions. These sparks are the primordial worlds, which could not continue, because the Sacred Aged had not as yet assumed his form (of opposite sexes—the King and Queen), and the Master was not yet at his work." And again we read (III, 61b) : "The Holy One, blessed be he, created and destroyed several worlds before the present one was made, and when this last work was nigh completed, all the things of this world, all the creatures of the universe, in whatever age they were to exist, before they entered into this world, were present before God in their true form. Thus are the words of Ecclesiastes to be understood. 'The thing that hath been, it is that which shall be; and that which is done is that which shall be done.' "

Since the Cabalists viewed all things from the anthropological point of view, they also transformed to the world of the Sephiroth the difference of sex. The male principle, called *Abba,* is white and of an active nature, appearing especially in the Sephirah Love, but also at the bottom of the three Sephiroth on the right side. The female principle, on the other hand, which owes its origin to the male principle, is red and of a receptive nature. It is mainly visible in the Sephira Justice, but is also at the bottom of the three Sephiroth on the left. The sign of the male principle is the "Y," that of the female the "H" in the divine name YHVH. What we learn is this: the Sephiroth teach that everything which exists is imperishable and like God. As nothing perishes in the world or is fully annihilated, thus the stamp and seal of divinity is stamped on all beings. God as the Invisible and Endless (En Soph) became visible and intelligible by the Sephiroth; the human mind can come to him, can know and conceive him.

The Realm of Evil.—Besides the heavenly realm of the Sephiroth of light or of the good, there is also a realm of the Sephiroth of darkness or of evil. Over against the supreme emanation of light, the Adam Kadmon, stands as opponent the Adam Belial. The same is the case with every light-sephirah, it is opposed by a Sephirah of darkness. Thus both are related to one another as the right side to the left; the light-Sephiroth form the right side, the darkness-Sephiroth the left side (*sitra achra*). The realm of darkness is figuratively called also the kingdom of Cain, Esau and Pharaoh (Zohar, I, 55*a*). Like the kingdom of light that of darkness has ten degrees. As the kingdom of light is inhabited by good spirits, so the kingdom of darkness is inhabited by evil spirits (demons, shells). Their prince is called Samaël (angel of poison or of death) ; his wife is called the Harlot or the Woman of Whoredom. Both are thought of as having intercourse with each other just as in the realm of light God as king has intercourse with Malchuth as queen. Through the influence of the evil powers the creation is continually disturbed. Men are seduced to apostasy from God, and thus the kingdom of the evil grows and the Keliphoth or shells increase. In the figurative language of the Zohar this disturbance of the creation is described as if the king and queen kept aloof from each other and could not work together for the welfare of the world. But this discord is finally harmonized by repentance, self-mortification, prayer and strict observance of the prescribed ceremonies, and the original harmony of things is again restored. It must be observed however that the teaching about the opposition of the two kingdoms belongs to the later doctrines of the Cabala and its development belongs to the thirteenth century.

Closely connected with the doctrine about evil is that of the Messiah. His coming takes place when the kingdom of the Keliphoth is overcome through the pious and virtuous life of men here on earth; then also takes place the restoration of the original state of affairs (*tikkun*). Since under his rule everything turns to the divine light, all idolatry ceases, because the Keliphoth no lónger seduce men to apostasy. Cabala as mistress, rules then over the slave philosophy. In the upper world, too, great changes take place at the coming of the Messiah. The king again has intercourse with the queen. Through their copulation the divinity regains the destroyed unity. But Wünsche says that cabalistic literature, especially the Zohar, often describes this union of the king and the queen in terms bordering on shamelessness and shocking to decency and morals.

The whole universe, however, was not complete, and did not receive its finishing stroke till man was formed, who is the acme of creation, and the microcosm uniting in himself the totality of beings.[9] The lower man is a type of the heavenly Adam Kadmon.[10] Man consists of body and soul. Though the body is only the raimant or the covering of the soul, yet it represents the *Merkaba* (the heavenly throne-chariot). All members have their symbolic meaning. Greater than the body is the soul, because it emanates from the En Soph and has the power to influence the intelligible world by means of channels (*zinnoroth*) and to bring blessings upon the nether world. The soul is called *nephesh*, "life," *ruach*, "soul," and *neshâmâ*, "spirit." As *neshama*,

[9] Zohar, III, 48*a*.
[10] Zohar, II, 70*b*.

which is the highest degree of being, it has the power to come into connection with God and the realm of light; as *ruach* it is the seat of good and evil; as *nephesh* it is immediately connected with the body and is the direct cause of its lower functions, instincts, and animal life.

Psychology.—Like Plato, Origen, etc., the Cabala teaches a pre-existence of the soul.[11] All souls destined to enter into human bodies existed from the beginning. Clad in a spiritual garb they dwell in their heavenly abode and enjoy the view of the divine splendor of the Shechinah. With great reluctance the soul enters into the body, for as Zohar, II, 96*b*, tells us, the soul, before assuming a human body, addresses God: "Lord of the Universe! Happy am I in this world, and do not wish to go into another where I shall be a bondmaid, and be exposed to all kinds of pollutions." Here, too, we notice again the influence of Platonic and Philonian doctrines. In its original state each soul is androgynous, and is separated into male and female when it descends on earth to be born in a human body. At the time of marriage both parts are united again as they were before, and again constitute one soul

---

[11] Compare Book of Wisdom, VIII, 20; Josephus, *Bell. Jud.*, II, 12, speaks of the Essenes as believing in a pre-existence of the soul. Philo's views are given in his *De somniis*, I, 642; *De gigantibus*, I, 263 f.

(Zohar, I, 91*b*). This doctrine reminds us of Plato and Philo no less than that other (viz. of ἀνάμνησις) that the soul carries her knowledge with her to the earth, so that "every thing which she learns here below she knew already, before she entered into this world" (Zohar, III, 61*b*). Of great interest is the metempsychosis of the Cabala. How this doctrine, already espoused by the Egyptians, Pythagoreans and Plato, came into Jewish mysticism, is not yet fully explained.[12] But it is interesting to learn of the destiny of man and the universe according to the Cabalists.

It is an absolute condition of the soul to return to the Infinite Source from which it emanated, after developing on earth the perfections, the germs of which are implanted in it. If the soul, after assuming a human body, fails during its first sojourn on earth to acquire that experience for which it descends from heaven, and becomes contaminated by sin, it must re-inhabit a body again and again, till it is able to ascend in a purified state. This transmigration or *gilgul,* however, is restricted to three times. "And if two souls in their third residence in human bodies are still too weak to resist all earthly trammels and to

[12] According to Josephus (*Antiq.,* XVIII, 13; *Bell. Jud.,* II, 8, 14) it would seem as if the Pharisees held the doctrine of the metempsychosis, but see Schürer, *Geschichte des jüdischen Volkes,* vol. II (3d ed., 1898) p. 391; on Philo's view, see *ibid.,* vol. III, p. 561.

acquire the necessary experience, they are both united and sent into one body, so that they may be able conjointly to learn that which they were too feeble to do separately. It sometimes happens, however, that it is the singleness and isolation of the soul which is the source of the weakness, and it requires help to pass through its probation. In that case it chooses for a companion a soul which has more strength and better fortune. The stronger of the two then becomes as it were the mother; she carries the sickly one in her bosom, and nurses her from her own substance, just as a woman nurses her child. Such an association is therefore called pregnancy (*ibbur*), because the stronger soul gives as it were life and substance to the weaker companion."

This doctrine of the *Superfoetatio* was especially taught by Isaac Loria or Luria. It is obvious that this doctrine of the Ibbur naturally led to wild superstition and fraudulent thaumaturgy. Loria himself claimed to have the soul of the Messiah ben Joseph. Connected with Loria's system is the doctrine of the Kawânâ, by which is meant the absorbed state of the soul in its direction towards God when performing the ceremonies, in prayer, self-mortification, in the pronunciation of the divine name and reading of the Zohar, whereby the bounds are broken and the fulness of blessing from the upper world is brought down upon the lower.

The world, being an expansion of the Deity's own substance, must also share ultimately that blessedness which it enjoyed in its first evolution. Even Satan himself, the archangel of wickedness, will be restored to his angelic nature, since he, too, proceeded from the Infinite Source of all things. When the last human soul has passed through probation, then the Messiah will appear and the great jubilee year will commence, when the whole pleroma of souls (*otzar ha-nesha-moth*), cleansed and purified shall return to the bosom of the Infinite Source and rest in the "Palace of Love" (Zohar, II, 97*a*).

Mystic Interpretation.—The exegetical ingenuity of the Cabala is interesting to the theologian. The principle of the mystic interpretation is universal and not peculiar to one or another school, as every one will perceive in ecclesiastical history, and even in the history of Greek literature. We find it in Philo, in the New Testament, in the writings of the fathers, in the Talmud, and in the Zohar; and the more such an interpretation departed from the spirit of the sacred text, the more necessary was it to bring the scriptures to its support by distortions of their meanings.[13]

[13] For a strange interpretation of scripture in modern times, the reader is referred to Canon Wordsworth's

Passing over all manner of subtleties of the pre-Zoharic times, we will consider the masterly performances of the Cabalists. According to them the letters, words and names of the scriptures contain divine mysteries of wondrous, mystical thoughts and ideas, of significant symbols and riddles, on which depends the continuance of the world. (Zohar, II, 99*a*). "Is it conceivable," the Zohar makes one of Simon ben Jochaï's circle exclaim, "that God had no holier matters to communicate than these common things about Esau and Hagar, Laban and Jacob, Balaam's ass, Balak's jealousy of Israel, and Zimri's lewdness? Does a collection of such tales, taken in their ordinary sense, deserve the name of Torah? And can it be said of such a revelation that it utters the pure truth? If that is all the Torah contains, we can produce in our time a book as good as this, aye, perhaps better. No, no! the higher, mystical sense of the Torah is its true sense. The biblical narratives resemble a beautiful dress which enraptures fools so that they do not look beneath it. This robe, however, covers a body, i. e., the precepts of the Law, and this again a soul, the higher soul. Woe to the guilty, who assert that the Torah contains only simple stories, and therefore look only upon the dress. Blessed are the righteous, who seek the real sense of the

Commentary on Genesis and Exodus, London, 1864, p. 52.

Law. The jar is not the wine, so stories do not make up the Torah" (*ibid.*, III, 152*a*). Thus the Cabalists attached little importance to the literal sense; yet not a single iota was to be taken from it and nothing was to be added to it (*ibid.*, II, 99).

In order to elicit the mysteries from the scriptures, the Cabalists employed certain hermeneutical canons,[14] viz.:

1. *Gematria*,[15] i. e., the art of discovering the hidden sense of the text by means of the numerical equivalents of the letters. Thus from the Hebrew words והנה שלשה (*vehineh sheloshah*) translated "lo! three (men stood by him)" in Gen. xviii, 2, it is deduced that these three were the angels Michael, Gabriel and Raphael, because the letters yield the numerical value of 701, viz.

$$ו = 6 + ה = 5 + נ = 50 + ה = 5 + ש = 300 + ל = 30 + ש = 300 + ה = 5 = 701$$; and the same number yield the words אלו מיכאל גבריאל ורפאל, viz. $$א = 1 + ל = 30 + ו = 6 + מ = 40 + י = 10 + כ = 20 + א = 1 + ל = 30 + ג = 3 + ב = 2 + ר = 200 + י = 10 + א = 1 + ל = 30 + ו = 6 + ר = 200 + פ = 80 + א = 1 + ל = 30 = 701.$$

A like figuring we find in the Epistle of Barnabas, ch, ix, with reference to the 318 servants

[14] On the interpretation of the scriptures among the Jews in general, see my article s. v. "Scripture, Interpretation of, Jewish," in McClintock and Strong.

[15] The word is not like γεωμετρία, as Levy, *Neuhebr. Wörterbuch,* I, 324, thinks, but is derived from γραμματεία or γράμμα.

of Abraham, mentioned in Gen. xiv. 14. The author lays stress upon the fact that in the Hebrew the "eighteen" are mentioned first, and the "three hundred" afterwards. In the eighteen expressed by the Greek letters $I = 10$ and $H = 8$ he sees Jesus (ΙΗΣΟΥΣ), and in the three hundred he sees by the letter $T = 300$, the cross.

With this canon may be compared the "number-oracle," by means of which one can tell from the number of the letters of the name and the dates of the birth important years and days in the life of a man. Thus, for instance, Emperor William I, was born March 22, 1797; $3 + 22 + 1797 + 7$ (number of the letters of the name $= 1829$, the year of marriage; $1829 + 1 + 8 + 2 + 9 = 1849$, campaign to Baden; $1849 + 1 + 8 + 4 + 9 = 1871$, coronation as emperor; $1871 + 1 + 8 + 7 + 1 = 1888$, year of death. Napoleon III, born 4, 20, 1808; $4 + 20 + 1808 + 8$ (number of the letters of the name) $= 1840$, the *coup* at Boulogne; $1840 + 1 + 8 + 4 + 0 = 1853$, first year as emperor; $1853 + 1 + 8 + 5 + 3 = 1870$; end of his rule.[16]

2. *Notarikon* (from the Latin *notarius*, a short-hand writer, one who among the Romans belonged to that class of writers who abbreviated and used single letters to signify whole words),

---

[16] For a somewhat different mode compare *The Open Court*, Feb. 1909, p. 88.

is employed when every letter of a wórd is takeń as an initial or abbreviation of a word. Thus, for instance, every letter of the Hebrew first word in Genesis,[17] is made the initial of a word, and from "in the beginning" we obtain "in the beginning God saw that Israel should accept the law"; or the word "Adam" (ADM) is made "Adam, David, Messiah." Sometimes very curious and ingenious combinations are derived from this system. For instance the word *passim*[18] used in the passage "And he made a coat of (*passim*) many colors" (Gen. xxxvii. 3) is made to indicate the misfortunes which Joseph experienced in being sold by his brethren to Potiphar, Merchants, Ishmaelites, Midianites.[19]

It appears that the Christian fathers sometimes made use of the same rule; as for instance Christ has been called by them ΙΧΘΥΣ, "fish," because these letters are the initials of the Greek words "Jesus Christ, the Son of God, the Saviour."[20] Thus St. Augustine tells us (*De civ. Dei*, XVIII, 23) that when they were speaking about Christ, Flaccianus, a very famous man, of most ready eloquence, and much learning, produced a Greek manuscript, saying that it was the prophecies of

---

[17] בראשית

[18] פסים

[19] פ=Potiphar, ס=Sochrim (merchants), י=Ishmaelites, מ=Midianites.

[20] Ἰησοῦς Χριστός, Θεοῦ Υἱός, Σωτήρ.

the Erythrian sibyl. In this he pointed out a certain passage that had the initial letters of the lines so arranged that those words could be read in them. Then he went on and gave these verses, of which the initial letters yield that meaning, and says, "But if you join the initial letters of these five Greek words, they will make the word *ichthus*,[21] that is 'fish,' in which word Christ is mystically understood, because he was able to live, that is, to exist, without sin in the abyss of this mortality as in the depth of waters." It is worthy of notice that Augustine only gives twenty-seven lines[22] of the thirty-four, as contained in the *Oracula Sibyllina*, VIII, 217 ff., where the acrostic reads: Jesus Christ, Son of God (the) Saviour, (the) Cross.[23] In its full form it is also given by Eusebius in the *Life of the Blessed Emperor Constantine*. For the benefit of the reader we subjoin Neale's translation of the acrostic as given in the *Christian Remembrancer*, October, 1861, p. 287:

"Judgment at hand, the earth shall sweat with
    fear.
Eternal king, the Judge shall come on high;
Shall doom all flesh; shall bid the world appear

[21] ἰχθύς.

[22] English translation by M. Dodd, *City of God,* Edinburgh, 1871, where the Greek letters at the beginning of the lines are retained.

[23] σταυρός.

88

Unveiled before his Throne. Him every eye
Shall, just or unjust, see in majesty.

"Consummate time shall view the Saints assemble
His own assessors, and the souls of men
Round the great judgment seat shall wait and
    tremble
In fear of sentence, and the green earth then
Shall turn to desert. They that see that day
To moles and bats their gods shall cast away.

"Sea, earth, and heaven, and hell's dread gates
    shall burn;
Obedient to their call, the dead return;
Nor shall the judge unfitting doom discern.

"Of chains and darkness to each wicked soul:
For them that have been good, the starry pole.

"Gnashing of teeth, and woe, and fierce despair
Of such as hear the righteous Judge declare
Deeds long forgot, which that last day shall bare.

"Then when each darkened breast He brings to
    sight,
Heaven's stars shall fall, and day be changed to
    night;
Effaced the sun-ray, and the moon's pale light.

"Surely the valleys He on high shall raise;
All hills shall cease, all mountains turn to plain;
Vessels shall no more pass the watery ways;
In the dread lightning parching earth shall blaze,
Ogygian rivers seek to flow in vain.
Unutterable woe the trumpet blast,
Re-echoing through the ether, shall forecast.

"Then Tartarus shall wrap the world in gloom,
High chiefs and princes shall receive their doom,
Eternal fire and brimstone for their tomb.

"Crown of the world, sweet wood, salvation's
    horn,
Rearing its beauty, shall for man be born,
O wood, that Saints adore, and sinners scorn!
So from twelve fountains shall its light be
    poured;
Staff of the Shepherd, and victorious sword."

We may also state that words of those verses
which are regarded as containing a peculiar recondite meaning are ranged in squares in such a
manner as to be read either vertically or boustrophedonally beginning at the right or left hand.
Again the words of several verses are placed over
each other, and the letters which stand under each
other are formed into new words. This is
especially seen in the treatment of three verses in

Exod. xiv. 19-21 (each containing 72 letters), which are believed to contain the three Pillars of the Sephiroth and the Divine Name of seventy-two words. Now, if these three verses be written out one above the other, the first from right to left, the second from left to right, and the third from right to left, they will give 72 columns of three letters each. Then each column will be a word of three letters, and as there are 72 columns, there will be 72 words of three letters, each of which will be the 72 names of the Deity. By writing the verses all from right to left, instead of boustrophedonally, there will be other sets of 72 names obtainable. The reader who is interested in these niceties will find ample information in Bartolocci, *Bibliotheca Magna Rabbinicia,* IV, pp. 230 ff.

3. *Temurah* or permutation.—According to certain rules, one letter is substituted for another letter preceding or following it in the alphabet, and thus from one word another word of totally different orthography may be formed. Thus the alphabet is bent exactly in the middle, and one half is put over the other; and then by changing alternately the first letter or the first two letters at the beginning of the second line, twenty-two permutations are produced. These are called the "Table of the Combinations of Tziruph."

For example's sake we give the method called Albath, thus:

A B G D H V Z Ch T Y K

L Th Sh R Q Tz P Ay S N M

The method abgath is thus exemplified:

A G D H V Z Ch T Y K L

B Th Sh R Q Tz P Ay S N M

The names of the twenty-two permutations are: Albath, Abgath, Agdath, Adbag, Ahbad, Avba, Azbav, Achbaz, Atbach, Aibat, Achbi, Albach, Ambal, Anbam, Asban, Aaybas, Afba, Azbaf, Akbaz, Arbak, Ashbar, Athbash. To these must be added as (23) Abgad; (24) Albam.

I will only remark that by the system called Athbash, it is found that the word *Sheshhach* in Jer. xxv. 26 is the same as Babel, and that Jerome is said to have confidently applied this system.[24]

Besides these canons the Cabala also sees a recondite sense in the form of the letters, as well as in the ornaments which adorn them. The more multifarious these trifles, the easier it is to arrive in every given case at a result, and the less wit or thought is required.

Although the canons mentioned above are already applied in the Talmud and Midrash, the Cabalists made a more copious use of them. The names of God became a special object of their fancy. With them they imagined they could accomplish everything and perform miracles, heal

---

[24] Hottinger possessed an entire Pentateuch explained on the principle of Athbash.

the sick, extinguish the fire, etc. The most miraculous effects were ascribed to the Tetragrammaton. Whoever was in possession of the true pronunciation of that name could enter in relation with the upper world and receive revelations. Each letter of the sacred name was considered as something mysterious. The letter Y (of YHVH) referred to the father as creator (*abba*) and H to the mother (*imma*). Because the letter H occurred twice, they distinguished an upper and a lower mother. The permutation of the letters of the Tetragrammaton brought about a multitude of new divine names which, either spoken or written, influenced the course and laws of nature. As was the case with the name of God consisting of four letters, so it was with that consisting of twelve, twenty-two, forty-two and seventy-two letters. All were believed to contain great mysteries.[25] The names of angels were treated in like manner. Thus the Cabalists greatly misused the Old Testament, especially the Thora. And, as says Professor Wünsche, by making the Bible a text-book to elicit deeper ideas, the greatest nonsense and rubbish came to light. The so-called hidden mysteries and revelations were nothing but fancies whirling in the heads of the Cabalists. The exe-

[25] Compare what we stated above in connection with Abulafia.

getical literature of the Cabala clearly proves that its representatives had completely lost the sense for a suitable understanding of the words of scripture.[26]

[26] A somewhat different view on the cabalistic treatment of scripture is given by the late Jewish scholar Zunz (died 1886) in his *Gottesdienstliche Vorträge* (Berlin, 1832), p. 403: For the passage in English see my article "Scripture Interpretation" in McClintock and Strong, vol. IX, p. 480.

CHAPTER VI.

THE CABALA IN RELATION TO JUDA-
ISM AND CHRISTIANITY.

Judaism.—It must be acknowledged that the Cabala intended to oppose philosophy and to intensify religion. But by introducing heathenish ideas it grafted on Judaism a conception of the world which was foreign to it and produced the most pernicious results. In place of the monotheistic biblical idea of God, according to which God is the creator, preserver and ruler of the world, the confused, pantheistically colored heathenish doctrine of emanation was substituted. The belief in the unity of God was replaced by the decade of the ten Sephiroth which were considered as divine substances. By no longer addressing prayers directly to god, but to the Sephiroth, a real Sephiroth-cult originated. The legal discussions of the Talmud were of no account; the Cabalists despised the Talmud, yea, they considered it as a canker of Judaism, which must be cut out if Judaism were to recover. Ac-

cording to the Zohar, I, *27b*; III, *275a*; *279b*,
the Talmud is only a bondmaid, but the Cabala a
controlling mistress.

The Cabalists compared the Talmud to a hard,
unfruitful rock, which when smitten yields only
scanty drops that in the end become a cause of
controversy; whereas the study of the Cabala is
like a fresh gushing spring, which one needs only
to address to cause it to pour out its refreshing
contents.[1]

And as the Cabalists treated the Talmud, they
likewise treated philosophy, which defined religious ideas and vindicated religious precepts before the forum of reason. Most Cabalists opposed philosophy. She was the Hagar that must
be driven from the house of Abraham, whereas
the Cabala was the Sarah, the real mistress. At
the time of the Messiah the mistress will rule
over the bondmaid.

But the study of the Bible was also neglected.
Scripture was no longer studied for its own sake,
but for the sake of finding the so-called higher
sense by means of mystical hermeneutical rules.

Even the rituals were variously changed and
recast. The putting on of the phylacteries and

---

[1] A collection of passages abusing the Talmud is
given by Landauer in the *Orient*, 1845, pp. 571-574; see
also Rubin, *Heidenthum und Kabbala,* Vienna, 1893, pp.
13 f.; also his *Kabbala und Agada, ibid.*, 1895, p. 5, where
we read that according to Abulafia the Cabalists only
were genuine men, and the Talmudists monkeys.

prayer-mantle (*talith*) was accompanied by the recitation of cabalistic formulas and sentences; special prayers were also addressed to the Sephiroth. Connected with all this was an extravagant, intoxicating superstition. To enable the soul to connect itself with the realm of light and its spirits, or to be transplanted after death into its heavenly abode, one underwent all manner of austere ascetical exercises. With the mysterious name of God they believed themselves enabled to heal the sick, to deliver demoniacs and to extinguish conflagrations. By application of the right formulas of prayer, man was to have power and influence on both the kingdoms of light and darkness. When the Cabalist prays, God shakes his head, changes at once his decrees, and abolishes heavy judgments. The magical names of God can even deliver the condemned and free them from their torments in their place of punishment. In this respect we even meet with the doctrine of the Catholic mass for the souls.[2] The Book of Psalms with its songs and prayers was especially considered as a means of producing all manner of miracles and magic, as may be seen from the *Sepher Shimmush Thehillim* (lit-

[2] Wünsche, whom we have followed, evidently refers to the prayer called Kaddish, for which see my article *s. v.* in McClintock and Strong, vol. XII. A very interesting article on "Jüdische Seelenmesse und Totenanrufung" is given by Dalman in *Saat auf Hoffnung* (Leipsic, 1890), pp. 169-225.

erally, "the Book of the Cabalistic Application of the Psalms"), a fragment of the practical Cabala, translated by Gottfried Selig, Berlin, 1788.

This sketch of Professor Wünsche is by no means exaggerated.[3] *Mutatis mutandis* we find the cabalistic notions among the Chasidim, a sect founded in 1740 by a certain Rabbi Israel ben Eliezer Baalshem,[4] also called Besht. Baal-Shem made his public appearance about 1740 in Tlusti, in the district of Czartkow, from whence he subsequently removed to Medziboze, in Podolia. The miraculous cures and prophecies attracted attention in large circles; his mode of life, consisting of contemplation, study of the Zohar and frequent washings in rivers, soon spread a halo around him. Added to this were the many miraculous reports circulated by his disciples; for instance, that his father had been visited by the prophet Elijah to predict his birth, and that his mother was a hundred years old when she was delivered of him; that, when a youth, he had victoriously struggled with evil spirits, etc.—all of

[3] Orelli in his article "Zauberei" in *Realencyklopädie für protest. Theologie und Kirche,* vol. XXI, 1908, p. 618, remarks: "The Jewish Cabala has promoted the magic degeneration of the religion; to a great extent it furnished profound expressions and formulas for the exercise of superstitious arts."

[4] "Lord of the name" = θεούργος, a man who by words of conjuration and other formulas knows how to exercise a power over the visible and invisible world.

which may be found in the Book *Shibche ha-Besht,* published in 1815 by the grandson of Baal-Shem, Rabbi Bär Linz. Baal-Shem[5] and his successors received the name *Tsaddik,* "Saint," and his fame attracted multitudes of Jews from all parts of Poland, who submitted themselves to his guidance. As long as he lived, the sect formed one great whole, of which he was the head. After his death, which took place in 1780, it was divided into separate congregations, each of which had its own Rabbi or Tsaddik or Saint, unreserved devotion to whom is the most important of all the principles of the sect. In a word, before Pius IX was declared infallible, the Chasidim[6] already had their infallible popes, whose number is still very large in Poland, Wallachia, Moldavia, Galicia, and Palestine. Of these popes of the Chasidim, a modern Jewish writer, the late David Cassel (died 1893), says: "To the disgrace of Judaism and modern culture the Tsaddikim still go on with their disgraceful business, and are thus the most essential hindrances to the dissemination of literary progress in Galicia and Russia. There are still thousands who

[5] Compare Kahana, *Rabbi Israel Baal Schem-Tob, sein Leben, kabbalistisches System und Wirken,* Sitomir, 1900.

[6] Compare Perl, *Megalleh temirin,* or *Die enthüllten Geheimnisse der Chassidim,* Lemberg, 1879; Ch. Bograt-schoff, *Entstehung, Entwicklung und Prinzipien des Chassidismus,* Berlin, 1908.

behold in the Tsaddik the worker of miracles, the prophet, one who is in close communion with God and angels, and who present him with rich gifts and promulgate the wonders which they have seen. Covetousness on the one hand and spiritual narrowness on the other are the channels through which the evil is fed anew."

Christianity.—As soon as the Cabala became better known, Christians betook themselves to its study and paid it the greatest attention because of the supposed agreement of its teachings with the dogmas of the Christian church. It was thought that the Cabala was the connecting link between Judaism and Christianity. The dogmas of the Trinity, of the Messiah as the Son of God and his atonement, were the salient points which especially attracted attention. The first to be drawn to the Cabala was Raymond Lully, the "Doctor Illuminatus" (1236-1315). He regarded the Cabala as a divine science and as a genuine revelation whose light is revealed to a rational soul.

The progress of Christianity towards the Cabala was greatly helped by the conversion of a large number of Jews to Christianity, "in which they recognized a closer relation to their gnostic views, and also by the Christians perceiving that gnosticism could become a powerful instrument for the conversion of the Jews." Among the

converted Jews we notice Paulus de Heredia of
Aragon (about 1480), author of *Iggeret ha-So-
dot* or *Epistola Secretorum,* treating of the divinity, death, and resurrection of the Messiah,
which has been ascribed to a certain Nechunjah
ben-ha-Kanah, who lived towards the end of the
second Temple.   Another convert was Paul
Ricci,[7] of the sixteenth century, the friend of
Erasmus, and physician to the Emperor Max-
imilian I; Julius Conrad Otto, author of the "Unveiled Secrets," consisting of extracts from the
Talmud and the Zohar, to prove the validity of
the Christian doctrine (Nuremberg, 1805); John
Stephen Rittengel, grandson of the celebrated
Isaac Abravanel, the translator of the Book Jezirah into Latin (Amsterdam, 1642).   Among
Christians we may mention Count John Pico di
Mirandola (born in 1463), author of *LXXII
conclusiones cabbalisticae,* Rome, 1486; more
especially John Reuchlin (Capnio), 1455-1522.
Reuchlin, the first German scholar who studied
the Cabala, wrote two cabalistic treaties, entitled
De Verbo Mirifico (Basel, 1494), and *De Arte
cabbalistica* (Hagenau, 1516).[8]

The first treatise is written in the form of a

---

[7]See my article *s. v.* in McClintock and Strong.

[8]These and some other treatises of the same kind
are collected by Pistorius in a collection entitled *Artis
cabbalisticae scriptores,* Basel, 1587.

dialogue between an Epicurean philosopher named Sidonius, a Jew named Baruch, and the author, who is introduced by the Greek name Capnio. Capnio would have it that the doctrine of the Trinity is to be found in the first verse of Genesis. He submits, if the Hebrew word *bra* (*bara*), which is translated "created," be examined, and if each of the three letters composing this word be taken as the initial of a separate word, we obtain the expression *ben, ruach, ab,* i. e., Son, Spirit, Father. Upon the same principle we find the two persons of the Trinity in the word *abn* (*eben*), "stone," occurring in Ps. cxviii. 22—"the stone which the builders rejected is become the head of the corner," by dividing the three letters composing the word *abn* into *ab ben,* i. e., Father, Son.

The second treatise is also in the form of a dialogue between a Mohammedan, a Pythagorean philosopher and a Jew. The dialogue is held at Frankfort where the Jew lives to whom the others come to be initiated into the mysteries of the Cabala. The whole is a more matured exposition and elaboration of the ideas hinted at in the first treatise.

How the truths of Christianity can be derived from the Talmud and the Cabala, the Franciscan Pietro Galatino endeavored to prove in his treatise *De Arcanis Catholicae Veritatis contra ob-*

stinatissimam Judaecorum nostrae tempestatis perfidiam (Ortona di Mare, 1518).

Much as Lully, Mirandola, Reuchlin, and others had already done to acquaint the Christian world with the secrets of the Cabala, none of these scholars had given translations of any portions of the Zohar. To this task Knorr Baron von Rosenroth betook himself by publishing the celebrated work *Kabbala Denudata* ("the Cabala Unveiled"), in two large volumes, the first of which was printed in Sulzbach, 1677-78, the second at Frankfort-on-the-Main, 1864, giving a Latin translation of the Introduction to and the following portion of the Sohar: the Book of Mysteries; the Great Assembly; the Small Assembly;[9] Joseph Gikatilla's Gate of Light (*shaar orah*); Vital's Doctrine of Metempsychosis (*hagilgulim*), and the Tree of Life (*etz chayim*); Cordovero's Garden of Pomegranates (*pardes rim-monim*); Abraham Herera's Gate of Heaven (*sha-ar ha shamayim*); Naphtali ben Jacob's Valley of the King (*emeq ha bacha*); Naphtali Cohen's Vision of the Priest (*maré Kohen*) etc., etc., with elaborate annotations, glossaries and indices. Knorr von Rosenroth has also collected all the passages of the New Testament which contain similar doctrines to those propounded by the Cabala. In spite of its many drawbacks[10] the

[9]These three parts are Englished by Mathers.
[10]Buddeus in *Introductio in Historiam Philosophiae*

work has been made use of by later scholars, especially by Chr. Schöttgen in his *Horae hebraicae et talmudicae* (Dresden, 1733) and *Theologia Judacorum de Messia* (*ibid.*, 1742.)

The powerful preponderance of the religious and ecclesiastical interests, as well as those of practical politics which became perceptible in the first quarter of the sixteenth century, giving to the mind a positive impulse, and to the studies a substantial foundation, arrested the further development of the Cabala; and thus it came about that in the course of time the zeal for cabalistic studies among Christians has cooled. It has become generally understood that the Cabala and Christianity are two different things. The idea of God according to the writings of the Old and New Testaments is entirely different. The same is the case with the notion of creation. When the first triad of the Sephiroth (Crown, Wisdom and Intelligence) is referred to the three persons of the Deity, their inner immanent relation is not thereby fully expressed, as Christianity teaches it. The three Sephiroth only represent three potencies of God or three forms of his emanation, the other Sephiroth are also such di-

Hebraeorum (Halle 1702) calls Knorr von Rosenroth's work "confusum et obscurum opus, in quo necessaria cum non necessariis utilia cum inutilibus, confusa sunt, et in unam velut chaos conjecta." Knorr von Rosenroth has also written a number of hymns.

vine powers and forms. One can therefore rightly say that the Cabala teaches not the Trinity, but the Ten-Unity of God. Also the other characteristics, when e. g. the Zohar ascribes to God three heads; or when it speaks of a God-Father (*abba*) of a God-Mother (*imma*) and of a God-Son; or when we are told (Zohar, III, 262*a*; comp. 67*a*) that "there are two, and one is connected with them, and they are three; but in being three, they are one," this does not coincide in the least with the Christian doctrine of the Trinity.[11]

In one codex of the Zohar we read on the words "Holy, holy, holy is the Lord of hosts" (Is. vi. 3): "the first 'holy' refers to the Holy Father; the second to the Holy Son; and the third to the Holy Ghost"; but this passage is now omitted from the present recensions of the Zohar, and has been regarded by some Jewish writers as an interpolation.[12]

As to the doctrine of Christ, the God incarnate —it cannot be paralleled with the confused doctrine of Adam Kadmon, the primordial man. Ac-

[11]Compare also Bischoff, *Die Kabbalah,* p. 26.

[12]Compare Joel, *Die Religionsphilosophie des Sohar,* Leipsic, 1849, pp. 240 ff.—The Zoharic passages referring to the Trinity are given in the original with a German translation in *Auszüge aus dem Buche Sohar* (by Tholuck; revised by Biesenthal), Berlin, 1857; 4th ed., 1876; also by Pauli, *The Great Mystery; or How Can Three Be One,* London, 1863.

cording to the Christian notion the reconciliation
is effected only through Christ, the Son of God;
according to the Cabala man can redeem himself
by means of a strict observance of the law, by as-
ceticism and other means whereby he influences
God and the world of light in a mystical manner.
For the benefit of the reader we give the following passages which speak of the atonement of the
Messiah for the sins of people, passages which
are given as the explanation of the fifty-third
chapter of Isaiah. "When the righteous are visited with sufferings and afflictions to atone for
the sins of the world, is that they might atone for
all the sins of this generation. How is this
proved? By all the members of the body. When
all members suffer, one member is afflicted in
order that all may recover. And which of them?
The arm. The arm is beaten, the blood is taken
from it, and then the recovery of all the members
of the body is secured. So it is with the children
of the world; they are members of one another.
When the Holy One, blessed be he, wishes the
recovery of the world, he afflicts one righteous
from their midst, and for his sake all are healed.
How is this shown? It is written—'He was
wounded for our transgressions, he was bruised
for our iniquities. . . .and with his stripes
we are healed' (Is. iii. 5)." Zohar, III, 218a.

To the same effect is the following passage:

"Those souls which tarry in the nether garden of Eden hover about the world, and when they see suffering or patient martyrs and those who suffer for the unity of God, they return and mention it to the Messiah. When they tell the Messiah of the afflictions of Israel in exile, and that the sinners among them do not reflect in order to know their Lord, he raises his voice and weeps because of those sinners, as it is written, 'he is wounded for our transgressions' (Is. liii. 5). Whereupon those souls return and take their place. In the garden of Eden there is one place which is called the palace of the sick. The Messiah goes into this palace and invokes all the sufferings, pain and afflictions of Israel to come upon him, and they all come upon him. Now if he did not remove them thus and take them upon himself, no man could endure the sufferings of Israel, due as punishment for transgressing the Law; as it is written—'Surely he hath borne our griefs and carried our sorrows,' etc. (Is. liii, 4 with Rom. xii. 3, 4). When the children of Israel were in the Holy Land they removed all those sufferings and afflictions from the world by their prayers and sacrifices, but now the Messiah removes them from the world." (Zohar, II, 212*b*). With reference to these passages[13] which speak of the

[13]A collection of the passages referring to the atoning work of the Messiah is given in *Auszüge aus dem*

atonement of the Messiah for the sins of the people, which are given in the Zohar as the explanation of the fifty-third chapter of Isaiah, Professor
Dalman[14] remarks that the Jews reject and object to cabalistic statements as something foreign
to genuine Judaism. The theosophic speculations
of the Cabala are at least just as Jewish as the
religious philosophical statements of Bachja or
Maimonides; yes, it seems to us that the God of
revelation and of scripture is more honestly retained in the former than in the latter, where he
becomes a mathematical One without attribute
and thereby may satisfy a superficial reason, but
leaves the heart empty. That these Jewish thinkers, influenced by Aristotle, had no inclination to
find in Is. liii an expiating mediator, is only too
inexplicable. He, who by his own strength can
soar into the sphere of "intelligences" and thus
bring his soul to immortality, needs no mediator.
But we are concerned here not with a philosophical or theosophical thought-complex, but the
simple question whether the prophet speaks in
Is. liii of a suffering mediator of salvation. The

Buche Sohar, pp. 35 f., more especially in Wünsche, Die
Leiden des Messias, Leipsic, 1870, pp. 95-105; and by
Dalman, "Das Kommen des Messias nach dem Sohar"
(in Saat auf Hoffnung), Leipsic, 1888, pp. 148-160.

[14]In his Jesaja 53, das Prophetenwort von Sühnleiden
des Heilandes mit besonderer Berücksichtigung der
synagogalen Literatur, Leipsic, 1890.

answer of the Cabalists at any rate agrees with the testimony of many of them.

What are we to think of the Cabala? That there is a relationship between it and neo-Platonism is obvious. Erich Bischoff[15] thinks that the Cabala represents a peculiar monism, which in some degree has influenced modern philosophy. In ethical respects it contains many fruitful and sublime thoughts, often indeed in fanciful wording. But as magic it has been of great influence on all kinds of superstitions and even on occultistic tendencies. It offers a highly interesting object of study whose closer investigation is rendered more difficult on account of the abtruse manner of representation and the many magic and mystic accessories. But that which is valuable is sufficient to insure for it a lasting interest.

[15]The author of *Die Kabbalah. Einführung in die jüdische Mystik und Geheimwissenschaft*, Leipsic, 1903.

BIBLIOGRAPHY.

The following references are given for the sake of those who may be sufficiently interested in the subject to enter further into its details:

Wolf, *Bibliotheca Hebraea*, Vol. II, pp. 1191-1247, Hamburg, 1728.

Fürst, *Bibliotheca Judaica*, Vol. III, pp. 320-325, Leipsic, 1863.

Brucker, *Kurtze Fragen aus der philosophischen Historie*, Vol. IV., Ulm, 1733.

Kleaker, *Ueber die Natur und den Ursprung der Emanationslehre bei den Kabbalisten*, Riga, 1786.

Beer, *Geschichte und Meinungen aller bestandenen und noch bestehenden Sekten der Juden und der Geheimlehre oder Kabbalah*, 2 Vols., Brünn, 1823.

Molitor, *Philosophie der Geschichte oder über die Tradition*, 4 Vols., Münster, 1827-1853; 2d. ed., 1857.

Freystadt, *Philosophia cabbalistica; Ex fontibus primariis adumbravit atque inter se comparavit*, Königsberg, 1832; *Kabbalismus und Pantheismus*, ibid. 1832.

Tholuck, *De ortu Cabbalae*, Hamburg, 1837.

Hamberger, *die hohe Bedeutung der alt-*

jüdischen Tradition oder der sogenannten Kabbalah, Sulzbach, 1844 (a review of Molitor's work).

Lutterbeck, *die neutestamentlichen Lehrbegriffe,* Vol. 1., 1853.

Misses, *Zaphnath Paneach, Darstellung und Kritsche Beleuchtung der jüdischen Geheimlehre,* 2 parts. Cracow, 1862-63.

Lichtenberger, *Enclypédie des' sciences religieuses,* art. "Cabale," Vol. II, pp. 497 ff., Paris, 1878.

Bloch, *Geschichte der Entwickelung der Kabbala,* Trier, 1894.

Ehrenpreis, *Kabbalistische Studien,* Part 1., Frankfort-on-the-Main, 1895.

Vacant, *Dictionaire de théologie catholique,* Paris, 1899, ff., art. "Cabale," Vol. II, 1271-91.

Wünsche, art. "Kabbala" in *Herzog-Hauck Realencyklopädie für Protestantische Theologie und Kirche,* Vol. IX, Leipsic, 1901.

Bischoff, *die Kabbalah; Einführung in die jüdische Mystik und Geheimwissenschaft,* Leipsic, 1903 (treats the subject in a catechetical manner).

Schülein, art. "Kabbala" in *Kirchliches Handlexikon,* München, 1907, ff. Vol. II, 255-257.

We have purposely refrained from referring to the historical handbooks of D. Cassel, S. Bäck, G. Karpeles, etc., because they offer nothing new from a critical point of view; and for obvious reasons we make no mention of articles on the Cabala in English Cyclopaedias.

INDEX

Abraham, p. 21.
Abulafia, Abraham, 40; tries to convert Pope Martin IV, 42; imagines himself the Messiah, 42.
Abulafia, Todros, 39.
Adam, book of, 33.
Agobard, 20.
Akiba, alphabet of, 18.
Allen, 4.
Arithmetic, theosophical, 22 et seq.
Augustine, 87.
Azariel, 33, 67.

Baal-shem, 98.
Bahir-book, teaches metempsychosis, 35.
Barnabas, 85.
Bartolocci, 15, 58, 91.
Basnage, 3.
Beer, 22.
Biesenthal, 105.
Bischoff, 105, 109.
Bodenschatz, 18.
Boehme, 3.
Bogratschoff, 99.
Bonwetsch, 22.
Buddéus, 104.

Cabala, name, 9; origin, 12; development, 16; most important doctrines concerning men and creation, 66; the realm of evil, 77; psychology, 80; metempsychosis, 81; mystical interpretation, 83; hermeneutical canons, 85; its relation to Judaism, 95; to Christianity, 100; does not teach the Trinity, 105; nor the Christ of the Christians, 106.
Cassel, D., 99.
Cassel, P., 75.
Chasidim, a Jewish sect, 98.
Christ called Ichthys, 88.
Cordovero, 57.
Cyclop. of McClintock and Strong, 13, 36, 40, 50, 51, 57, 59, 61, 62, 63, 85, 94, 97, 101.

Dalman, 97, 108.
Dodd, 88.

Edersheim, 21.
Elisha ben-Abuja, 12.
En Soph, 34.
Emanations, treatise on the, 37.
Enoch, Book of, 19.
Etheridge, 4.
Eusebius, 22, 88.
Eybenschütz, 64.

Fludd, 3.
Franck, 5.
Frank, Jacob, 64.

Galatino, 102.
Geiger, 6.

INDEX

Gematria, 85.
Gikatilla, 42.
Gill, 4.
Ginsburg, 7.
God, His body described, 18; is endless according to the Cabala, 66; makes Himself known in the creation by means of ten Sephiroth or emanations, 67, 77; which are divided into groups and in this way yield three different forms as the diagrams show, 67; the emanations, representing the first manifestation of God form an ideal world; from which proceed by an emanation in different gradations four worlds, 74.
Goldschmidt, 21.
Graetz, 7, 52, 75.
Grünbaum, 22.
Günsburg, 40.

Helmont, 3.
Heredia, 101.
Horwitz, 60.
Hottinger, 92.

Interpretation, mystical, 83.
Isaac the Blind, 33; father of the Cabala, 34.
Ishmaël ben Elisa, 13.

Jehudah Halevi, 21.
Jellinek, 5, 6, 7, 17, 18, 19, 33, 37, 52.
Jezirah, book of, 20; time and place of composition, 20; contents, 21; theosophical arithmetic, 22.
Joel, 6, 105.
Josephus, 80.
Jost, 7.
Juchasin, 52.

Kahana, 99.
Kawana, doctrine of, 82.
Kircher, 18.

Landauer, 6, 96.
Latif Ibn, 39, 74.
Leon de Modena, 60, 61.
Letters, combination of, 30.
Longfellow, 38.
Lully, 3, 100.
Luria, 57, 58.
Luzzatto, 65.

Maasey Merkaba and Bereshit, 17.
Maimonides, 14; denounces mysticism, 19.
Man the acme of creation, 79.
Mathers, 8.
Medigo, Elias del, calls the Zohar a forgery, 57.
Messiah, His coming, 78; atonement of, 106.
Messiahship, 58; teaches superfoetatio, 82.
Metatron, 25, 38, 75.
Metempsychosis, 81.
Midrash Konen, 33.
Milman, 4.
Mirandola, 3, 55, 101.
More, 3.
Morinus, 51.
Moses de Leon, 5; author of the Zohar, 43.

Nachmanides, 36.
Nasir, 37, 74.
Neale, 88.
Nechunjah Ben-Ha-Kanah, 13, 35.
Nettesheim, 3.
Notarikon, 86.
Number, oracle, 86.

Ophanim, 24, 38.
Oracula Sibyllina, 88.

INDEX

Orelli, 98.
Origen, 80.
Ottó, 101.

Paracelsus, 3.
Pauli, 105.
Perl, 99.
Philo, 80, 81.
Picard, 61.
Pistorius, 101.
Plato, 80, 81.
Proclus, 67.

Reuchlin, 3, 101.
Ricci, 101.
Rittengel, 101.
Rosenroth, Knorr von, 43, 45, 58, 103.
Rubin, 96.

Sabbatai, Zebil, 61; proclaims himself the Messiah, embraces Islamism, 62; ruins thousands of Jewish families, 63.
Sachs, 6.
Samaël, prince of darkness, 77; his wife called the harlot, 78.
Sandalphon, 25, 38.
Schöttgen, 104.
Schürer, 81.
Scripture references:
    Genesis XIV, 14, 86; XXXVII, 3, 87.
    Exodus, XIV, 19-21, 91; XX, 20, 25.
    Ps. XXXIV, 18, 18; CXVIII, 22 102.
    Prov. III, 13, 38.
    Isa. VI, 2, 18; 3, 105; LIII, 4, 107; 5, 106, 107.
    Jer. XXV, 26, 92.

Ezek. I, 20, 24.
Rom. XII, 3, 4, 107.
Selig, 98.
Sephiroth, 25, 34, 38; opposed by a Sephirah of darkness, 77.
Seraphim, 24.
Simon ben Jochai, 4, 5; pre-existence of soul, 80.
Steinschneider, 6.
Stern, 7.
Strack, 50.
Superfoetatio, doctrine of, 82.
Sandolphon, 38.

Temurah, 91.
Tetra grammaton, 93.
Tholuck, 105.
Tziruph, 91.

Vital, continues work of Luria, 59; has many adherents, 60.

Wakkar, endeavors to reconcile the Cabala with philosophy, 55.
Westcott, 6.
Wordsworth, 84.
World, the present, the best, 75.
Wünsche, 20, 33, 93, 108.

Zohar, written by Moses de Leon, 43; its supplementary portions, 46; the late authorship proven from the reference to the Crusades and other events, 51; becomes the text-book of the Cabala, 54; its followers denounce the anti-Cabalists, 56.
Zunz, 6, 94.